LEARNING TO FLY

BOOKS BY MARY LEE SETTLE

The Love Eaters. New York: Harper, 1954.

The Kiss of Kin. New York: Harper, 1955.

O Beulah Land. New York: Viking, 1956.

Know Nothing. New York: Viking, 1960.

Fight Night on a Sweet Saturday. New York: Viking, 1964.

All the Brave Promises: Memories of Aircraft Woman 2nd Class 2146391. New York: Delacorte, 1966.

The Story of Flight. New York: Random House, 1967.

The Clam Shell. New York: Delacorte, 1971.

The Scopes Trial: The State of Tennessee v. John Thomas Scopes. New York: Watts, 1972.

Prisons. New York: Putnam, 1973.

Blood Tie. Boston: Houghton Mifflin, 1977.

The Scapegoat. New York: Random House, 1980.

The Killing Ground. New York: Farrar, Straus and Giroux, 1982 (to replace *Fight Night on a Sweet Saturday* as the final volume of the Beulah Quintet).

Water World. New York: Dutton, 1984.

Celebration. New York: Farrar, Straus and Giroux, 1986.

Charley Bland. New York: Farrar, Straus and Giroux, 1989.

Turkish Reflections: A Biography of a Place. New York: Prentice Hall, 1991.

Choices. New York: Doubleday, 1995.

Addie: A Memoir. Columbia: University of South Carolina Press, 1998.

I, Roger Williams: A Novel. New York: W. W. Norton, 2001.

Spanish Recognitions: The Roads to the Present. New York: W. W. Norton, 2004.

LEARNING TO FLY

A Writer's Memoir

Mary Lee Settle

Edited by Anne Hobson Freeman

W. W. NORTON & COMPANY
New York   London

Chapter 7, "London, 1944" adapted from "London, 1944."
Virginia Quarterly Review, Autumn 1987.
Chapter 11, "Mr. Eliot" adapted from "How Pleasant to Meet Mr. Eliot."
New York Times Book Review, December 16, 1984.
Chapter 14, "Maugham" adapted from "Maugham."
The Yale Review, spring 1987, vol. 76.

Every effort has been made to contact the copyright holder of each of the
selections. Rights holders of any selections not credited should contact
W. W. Norton & Company, Inc., 500 Fifth Avenue, New York, NY 10110, in order
for a correction to be made in the next printing of our work.

For information about permission to reproduce selections from
this book, write to Permissions, W. W. Norton & Company, Inc.,
500 Fifth Avenue, New York, NY 10110

For information about special discounts for bulk purchases, please contact
W. W. Norton Special Sales at specialsales@wwnorton.com or 800-233-4830.

Manufacturing by Courier Westford
Book design by Rhea Braunstein
Production manager: Anna Oler

Library of Congress Cataloging-in-Publication Data

Settle, Mary Lee.
Learning to fly : a writer's memoir / Mary Lee Settle ;
edited by Anne Hobson Freeman. — 1st ed.
p. cm.
ISBN 978-0-393-05732-4 (hardcover)
1. Settle, Mary Lee. 2. Authors, American—20th century—Biography.
I. Freeman, Anne Hobson, 1934– II. Title.
PS3569.E84Z46 2007
813'.54—dc22
[B]   2007023111

W. W. Norton & Company, Inc.
500 Fifth Avenue, New York, N.Y. 10110
www.wwnorton.com

W. W. Norton & Company Ltd.
Castle House, 75/76 Wells Street, London W1T 3QT

1 2 3 4 5 6 7 8 9 0

CONTENTS

❦

PART I
INTRODUCTION

"An autobiography that begins with one's birth begins too late," says Mary Lee Settle in *Addie*—an earlier memoir in which she interweaves the story of her grandmother, Addie Tompkins, the social history of the Kanawha Valley, and scenes from her own childhood in West Virginia.

Had she lived to put the final touches on this memoir, *Learning to Fly*, Settle might have offered an introduction to suggest the forces that had shaped, and were beginning to imprison, the stagestruck Barter Theatre intern we encounter on the first page of the first chapter.

Readers already familiar with Mary Lee Settle's life may have no trouble plunging into it midstream, but for others a preface has been constructed using blocks of text found in earlier drafts on her computer. Together they suggest the profound effect that the Depression had on Settle in her late childhood and early adolescence; on her grandmother, Miss Addie; and, in particular, on her parents.

In another fragment, Settle writes that even after her father had found enough work to move his family out of Addie's house at Cedar Grove to a rented house of their own, seventeen miles downriver in Charleston: "There were always five of us in that little house . . . my father, my mother, my brother, myself, and the Great Depression."

In the preface to *Addie*, Settle takes a longer view and writes: "I was formed by riverrun, east from Virginia, where the mountains cut us off from our past but not our memory, west to the Ohio, the Mississippi. I was formed by eons of earthquake, and the rise of the mountains and the crushing of swamps into coal as surely as by timid human copulation. Old choices, not my own, set me down in one place and not another."

In *Learning to Fly,* new choices, all her own, will fling her out into a wider, more challenging, and truly dangerous world. While she is racing through the roles of would-be actress, New York model, wartime bride, and young mother to become a signals operator with the Women's Auxiliary Air Force (WAAF) of the Royal Air Force at the height of World War II, the writer incubating within her, still virtually unnoticed, begins pecking at its shell.

It emerges timidly amid the buzz bombs and the V-2 rockets in London, after she is hired as a writer for the U.S. Office of War Information (OWI) by editors too hard-pressed in the rush toward D-Day to notice that she is, in fact, "a fake" with no experience.

Several years before her death in September 2005, at the age of eighty-seven, as her memory of earlier events became increasingly vivid and insistent, Mary Lee Settle felt a compulsion "to trace the way that led me into being the writer I have become."

The result is a refreshingly unsentimental journey through the years that led to her commitment to writing late in 1945 and nine years of hardship and apprenticeship before that choice was vindicated by the publication of *The Love Eaters* in 1954.

The action of this book begins in the summer of 1938. Preoccupied with the construction of her new house in the best section of Charleston, West Virginia, Settle's mother has decided to send her troublesome daughter away for a summer internship at the Barter Theatre—assuming that she will, of course, return for her junior year at Sweet Briar College in the fall.

For Mary Lee, who is just turning twenty, the summer will prove to be a crossroads at which she summons up the courage to take an unexpected turn—the first step on a road that will be rich in perils and adventure, laughter, sorrow, and hard-won wisdom, a road few women of her era would have dared to travel.

—Anne Hobson Freeman
  February 2007

PRELUDE TO THE SUMMER OF 1938

ᖰ~

I was going to become a classical actress, preferably Shakespearean. This was not, to me, a hope, but a fact. It had been my goal since I climbed the attic stairs at the Mason School of Music, when I was ten, and found Mr. Maurice Drew, an ex-actor. Maybe he had been flotsam from a showboat. I never knew what had marooned him in Charleston, West Virginia. I only know that a long road began with a climb up the stairs to the attic of the Mason School of Music. We studied Shakespeare together when my parents thought I was learning "pieces" and getting rid of what they had decided was a speech impediment. It was their conscious decision.

The overwhelming force behind it, never recognized, was that my mother was a woman who needed to be alone as desperately as others needed food. So Mr. Drew was my babysitter every Wednesday afternoon.

Then the miracles began to happen. Franklin Roosevelt was elected. Nobody who did not live through that time can imagine the impact of that election. My father was prosperous for the first time since the closing of the mine he had managed until I was six. He was hired by the Public Works Administration (PWA) as a civil engineer. Now he could help fight the Depression by

putting people to work, and he began to recover from the ago-
nizing *tic douloureux* that had hounded him for years.

Then there was the third miracle, which was not a miracle
except to my mother. The state of West Virginia condemned
the air over the family house at Cedar Grove, where my
mother's parents, and then, for years, her widowed mother,
Addie, had raised a family.

During the Depression, Miss Addie was a great tree under
which all her children, including my mother, found shelter.
Although she hadn't voted for Roosevelt, Miss Addie accepted
him, but she hated Henry Wallace, the secretary of agriculture,
because he had little pigs killed when people were hungry.

She herself kept a ten-gallon tin of milk on the back
porch—filled with the milk that my aunt Myrtle milked from
the Jersey cow she treated like a friend. And she told all the children up Horse Mill Hollow (where the tenant houses that had
once been slave cabins were) that they were to come and drink
as much as they wanted. Never in the Depression did she make
any tenant move for nonpayment of rent, but she did insist on
their planting vegetable gardens. She gave them the seed and
saw that they did right.

A highway ramp was to be built over what my grandmother
called her "piece of property," and my mother called "the
estate" at Cedar Grove. I guess it made it less painful for driv-
ers to fly over the little coal town where the tenant houses were
neglected, except when Miss Addie took hammer and nails and
fixed what she could. They sagged, human-looking and sad, as
if they had been left out in the rain.

With her share of the condemnation rights over Cedar
Grove—the property where Miss Addie, of whom she was
ashamed, still lived—my mother and my father had decided to
build a house.

All of Miss Addie's children and grandchildren had been raised at Cedar Grove. Most of my mother's hopes had been born there—as well as her dreams. The American dream of those who had suffered the indignity of having their choices made by others who did not know they existed. The hopes that had turned to those dreams, turned at last to plans. I had never seen my parents so happy, before or since that year when the condemnation rights and the security my civil-engineer father earned, by turning West Virginia from a state of outdoor privies to a state of flushed toilets, gave them hope.

Over the years, which were the years of my childhood and early adolescence, those dreams had taken my parents along a rocky road through mine closing, Florida boom busting, and homecoming with what my mother saw as their tails between their legs. Now the dreams were being turned into a house in a part of Charleston where she wanted to live.

It would be a Queen Anne house. They went to the newly revived Williamsburg to measure lintels and doors and take samples of paint. They took me with them from Sweet Briar, and I watched them from the garden of the Governor's Palace, contemplating suicide because I was caught in a scandal and a waste of spirit, about which I still dream, still apologizing, still telling anyone who will listen that I did nothing wrong.[1] Years later, I wrote about it in *The Clam Shell*. I was eighteen.

At last my mother would live on a piece of property they owned instead of renting, which she loathed. Owning acres was what she had been trained by her father to expect. He had also

---

[1] During her freshman year at Sweet Briar, in the early spring of 1937, Settle barely escaped an attempted "date rape." The insensitivity of the college administrators' response, their refusal to believe what she said, and her feeling that she had been mistreated and branded left her with a lifelong resentment of the college, although she did return to it for her sophomore year.—AHF.

trained his favorite child in every snobbery the small valley of the Kanawha could stand. My Civil War grandfather's training had gone into her blood, her dreams, and her backbone. It had failed to go into mine.

My father saw her begin to bloom again after the horrors of the Depression that no longer existed except in his worried, often-sleepless nights. For the rest of his life, he had what is now called *post-traumatic stress disorder*. Maybe that is why he was a Republican. He yearned to go back to the way things had been when children obeyed their parents and families were happy. What families and when I don't think ever came into his mind.

The condemnation rights and the PWA were the real foundations of the new house before a single hole was dug for a basement on a hillside lot that Miss Addie said you couldn't pasture a goat on, and into which they were pouring all of their pride, their new youth, now that the Depression, that haunting monster in every house, was being lifted at last.

Those of us who were children then, like people who have grown up in wartime, absorbed too much silent preoccupation that we remember as somehow our own fault, parents who had to say, "Can't afford it," dignified mothers crying in their bedrooms behind closed doors we didn't dare enter after telephone calls we knew were demands for payment from the grocery store.

My part in this dream-come-true was that my father insisted that I be sent to Sweet Briar, the nice place for nice girls who would marry nice boys and take at least a few wrinkles from their fathers' faces—Sweet Briar in Virginia, instead of Barnard, where I longed to go and had been accepted.

My departure for Sweet Briar and my brother's marriage to a young favorite of my mother's (in his lifelong yearning to please her, which he could only escape by getting drunk) some-how meant to my parents that they were free, if only for a little while, of parenthood.

They didn't demand; they wished wholeheartedly for all of the things that are supposed to happen, as formal as a dance: renewed quiet, a release of breath after the worst years of their and everybody's lives. It was a milestone that was being passed all over the country, the great American sigh of relief from the dark shadow that had ruined their lives.

Even though my father was a black Republican and my mother a yellow-dog Democrat, they and my brother and I had been saved by Franklin Delano Roosevelt.

1

FROM BARTER TO MANHATTAN

❧

On my twenty-first birthday I danced a Viennese waltz with Prince Serge Obolensky on the St. Regis Roof. I wore an ice-blue satin evening dress that had been bought for me to take to Sweet Briar. I was meant to go back for my junior year there. But I was sent to New York instead. It was, inadvertently, my mother's doing.

It had to do with condemnation rights, the PWA, and Franklin Roosevelt, all of which had, in the words of my Cedar Grove grandmother, Miss Addie, saved their bacon.

None of this seemed to affect me as the summer of 1938 began. I was busy getting on my mother's nerves downriver in Charleston. For her, I was an ever-present fingernail on a blackboard. She loved silence and being alone. I can understand that now, but then it was a wall I kept trying to climb, demanding that she, at least, notice me.

Only once did I succeed. One morning she noticed me enough to throw a shoe at me, the only time I ever saw her lose the cliff-edge poise she so needed in such a dark time. When the bedroom slipper hit my arm, I knew that she knew I was there. I have never forgotten it. For a little while, I respected and liked her.

Her dreams had clashed with mine, and there was nothing that she could do about it except ignore mine, control them, or put them down with a famous family wit that bit like a snake. Her dreams were finally coming true, and I was in their way.

I was nineteen. It was generally conceded by her friends and my father that I was driving her crazy. So she made plans to get me out of the way for the summer. She chose the Barter Theatre as a babysitter.

How was she to know that David O. Selznick had sent more than a hundred talent scouts to comb Virginia and the rest of the South for southern accents? She had thrown me, body and soul, into the briar patch.

Abingdon, Virginia, was, in those days, a town with one inn, one combined grocery store and bar, and one summer theater in a county of cornfields and cattle. The audiences could buy their tickets with barter; we ate a lot of ham and corn. Maybe the theater was small and poor then, but to me it was a daily heaven. As if all the action I had dreamed of on late hot nights when I couldn't sleep was real and happening, really happening. It was my first plunge into professional life of any kind, except that I had sold Christmas cards to earn the money to buy Christmas presents when I was ten and the Depression was in full terror.

Robert Porterfield and his wife had started the Barter Theatre during the Depression as well, so that actors from that holy of holies, New York, could eat all summer and act all summer and paint scenery all summer. I was expected to do the same, except for a class several times a week on the Moscow Art Theater's method of acting, which consisted of mime, confession, and, in my case, scene-stealing. I had already learned that when I was ten and played Robin, a page, in *The Merry Wives of Windsor*. The director had made the mistake of putting me down stage left and giving me a top to spin.

Almost every actor that summer at the Barter Theatre had worked, if only for a few performances, in a Broadway show, and all of them, without exception, knew every agent around Forty-fourth Street. They told me about the daily news at the Walgreen's drugstore on the corner of Forty-fourth and Broadway, where the word was passed. Casting.

Years later, I was told by Donald Ogden Stewart that you knew you had arrived when you could go to the back of the same Walgreen's drugstore, tap on a little square peephole, and say, "Benchley sent me." It had hidden one of the most fashionable speakeasies in New York.

I was cast in play after play that summer—sometimes bit parts, once a lead. We even toured the mountain resorts from South Carolina to Virginia. When I saw my Sweet Briar friends, I felt alien, and somehow beyond a pale I couldn't define. I was not "one of us" anymore. I had become "one of them." And I tried to love it, but I was only embarrassed at feeling grown-up, professional, and a half-defined outsider. I told myself that we, the new "we," were better off than our actor ancestors who were vagabonds by law and thrown in the sewer when they died, but that did little good. For the first time in my life, and God knows not the last, I realized the social asset of the power to hurt, an asset I had once possessed, had taken for granted, had even, at times, enjoyed.

There were two tryouts at Barter that summer. One was a musical. I was an old woman with a basket. I have no idea now why. The other was a play by Lula Vollmer, who had made a success on Broadway with *Sun-Up*. Robert Porterfield, like all the rest of the actors, was hoping for a Broadway lead from it. He played the title role in *The Dunce Boy*. It was an absolutely dreadful play.

Every character was familiar. I was the schoolteacher who

had come up into the mountains to educate the neglected hill-billies. That was the accepted do-gooder in the 1930s—save the mountaineers and learn their songs. It was the tail end of the great work of the Lomaxes, the influence of *The Grapes of Wrath*, and the long, long run of *Tobacco Road*. I found out that she had actually written a play on which was based a film with Katharine Hepburn, who for me lived next door to God. Called *Spitfire*, it was a total box-office failure. I saw it four times. So I had chills about being in the same room with Lula Vollmer, who had had a success on Broadway and who had met Katharine Hepburn.

In *The Dunce Boy*, there were the expected mountaineers, a mill owner, at least I think he was—a villainous exploiter who had, in the thirties, replaced the showboat dramas' musta-chioed landlord. The dunce boy, of course, fell in love with the schoolteacher.

So there I was on the stage at the Barter Theatre in a lead role; I had already begun to take for granted that this was what I had some secret right to expect. I learned to stay in character while kneeling in front of Bob Porterfield in the most intense scene of the play, while he employed the trick he had of shift-ing his upstage eye to try to break me up. It was a far cry from Shakespeare or George Bernard Shaw or Noel Coward, who stood, for me, at opposite ends of a series of plays where I could see myself starring.

In the last act of melodramatic nobility, the dunce boy sac-rificed himself to the sawmill to the background music of the opening of Tchaikovsky's Piano Concerto No. 1: boom boom boom boom da da da da, twiddle twiddle twiddle, da da da da. In the sixty-five years since, I have not been able to hear that opening without laughing.

Lula Vollmer came down to spend the summer at the

Barter. She was a large, middle-aged woman with a flaccid body that spread when she sat, or lounged, through rehearsals in the back of the house, issuing orders in a mountaineer boom. She had a huge bun of hair in a red that had never grown naturally on any head. It was sumac red, that first bright color as the mountains change in the fall.

We lived in sad, neglected rooms in wooden dormitories that were used by a normal school (teachers' college) in the winter months. One Sunday morning, I awoke to a wild wailing that seemed to come from the attic. People had come out into the hall to listen. Finally I could stand it no longer, and I crawled up the attic stairs.

There she was, Lula Vollmer, drunk on a Sunday morning, in her dressing gown with her bright red hair like a tent around her, fallen to the floor. She sat in a rickety chair in the dim sunlight of a dirty attic window. She had a bottle in one hand and a Bible in the other. She was singing Revivalist hymns that I had heard my grandmother, Miss Addie, sing all through my childhood. Lula Vollmer had gone to church.

So the Barter Theatre was my first lesson in professional acting and the unwritten rules that went with it—concentration, quick study, empathy without identity, which ensures control of the character, a whole-body awareness, a sensate memory, all of which I look back on now as some of the most valuable lessons as a writer I have ever had. The other milestone for me was my introduction to Richard Boleslavsky's *Acting: The First Six Lessons*, which has taught me more about the technique of writing fiction than anything, except a long and impatient study of every classic novel from the eighteenth century to Joseph Conrad and Marcel Proust.

That summer I acted, and studied, and had my first love affair. In *Choices*, Melinda gives away her virginity to a sad boy as a Christmas present. In my case it was a birthday present. I had just turned twenty.

I think it was in August that the scout from Selznick arrived. I remember him as if he were still standing there in front of me, but I do not remember his name. He looks, looked, like a movie detective—soft-brimmed hat, old raincoat, with a surprisingly kind face for one who represented Hollywood, and an accent that was part Brooklyn and part gravelly Wild West. He was a very nice man.

Rhett Butler's scene in the jail was what he must have read, over and over and over, in every southern state that summer. That was the script he gave me to read while he threw me cues in his down-and-dirty New York accent. "Lemme see ya hens." I wish I could remember his name. What I will never forget was his tenderness, I'm sure, with all the hopefuls he had to reject over and over that summer. He was easy, friendly, putting me at my ease, an ease that never happened. I was twittering within like a bird with tiny bones, hypnotized by him and by being noticed in this small center of a summer world by this milestone of a man whose name is gone.

One of the dim rooms on the first floor of the dormitory became a jail cell. I tried not to hear the whispers of my fellow actors outside the window. He still wore a raincoat, I think, because he kept his cigarettes in its pocket. He fed me Rhett Butler lines. I had been given about an hour to study the scene. I was Scarlett, not dressed in the velvet drawing-room draperies but in my paint-smeared overalls. It was the scene where Scarlett tried to borrow money from Rhett Butler. It is hard now to remember myself reading; it is a fact, not a memory, that I played the scene; I do remember being proud when flirting was demanded. I had never flirted with anybody in my life, although I had envied and learned protective contempt for

those who could. I was too tall. I had long since learned to
wheedle, though.

I wheedled.

All I see again in that room is the cheap, worn plywood
door. But together he and I managed to conjure up the atmosphere of a jail. We really did. When I opened the door and swept
out, the scout said, "Good, honey, that's good." He must have
said it a hundred times, all over the South that summer. I was
surprised at having passed the first test, and having won an
appointment to go to New York in the fall and read for the
New York casting director, which shows how desperate the
search for Scarlett was, and how far they were willing to go.

I went home with a complimentary ticket to New York in
my pocket and an introduction to the casting director in New
York, with a real appointment at a real time. I was suspended
partly in joy, partly in disbelief. I was afraid to tell my family. It
wasn't the noise they would make in argument. It was the
silence I feared most. It always had been.

Miss Katybelle for me is forever Mistress Quigley in *The
Merry Wives of Windsor*, but that summer she was also our landlady. My family had moved to her house on Kanawha Street by
the river while the house was being finished. I was stating my
integrity in the small back bedroom by putting a print of *The
Absinthe Drinker* by Toulouse-Lautrec on the wall, and my
mother was stating hers by exchanging it for a flower print and
hiding the record of the "Liebestod," sung by Flagstad and
Melchior, so she wouldn't have to hear it for the thousandth
time. Neither of us ever said a word about the print or the
music.

I remember standing there, waiting to have nerve enough
to speak, when my mother stopped in the open door and said,
"You are not going back to Sweet Briar, are you?" It did not sur-

prise me. She had read my mind. It wasn't the first time by a long shot, as I had learned over and over.

"No, ma'am," I said, which was the way I answered her until she died at ninety-two. Blind and bedridden, she was still the most frightening woman I have ever known.

I thought then, she approves, but she would never admit it because of my father. So, having investigated New York through nice people, including the governor, they settled on a women-only hotel on the West Side where there was a swimming pool. We made that formal crossing of the bridge to the C&O station that had for two years meant Sweet Briar, where some of the students kept horses and I had been like a colt myself, trying to run away.

That iron-lace bridge across the Kanawha River was my Rubicon, and I knew it, every minute of it, as we crossed, nobody saying a word or giving advice for once. I can still see my parents' backs, stiff with silence, as I sat in the seat behind them. I still dream sometimes, wherever I have been—a thousand miles, a continent, ocean years, away—of crossing that bridge, or trying and failing to cross it, and of taking friends to see the river, how beautiful it is.

My mother made sure I had what she called a decent wardrobe. My father said nothing. His dream of having a lovely daughter who went to Sweet Briar and married well had been shattered, and there was nothing he could do about it. His face was set like it was when Roosevelt was elected. He made sure I had enough money. It was the last thing he asked me.

In 1938, at the end of Park Avenue, the Grand Central Building was indeed a grand beacon against the sky. Now it looks diminished and protected by the huge building that towers behind it. It was there that I was ushered into an office, where Kaye Brown sat waiting. I couldn't have been there more than an hour until I was finished with Hollywood before I had begun. But it is still as if I had just walked through that door. I remember where she sat, how she looked, the light that came in the window on the right wall.

It was the first time Kaye Brown stepped into my life and out again. Years later, she was my literary agent. She was one of the truly benign people I was to meet and know in that rocky, deceptive world of the theater and later of publishing.

She advised me against taking a stock contract to go to Hollywood to be one of the Southern girls. "You might just get out there and be forgotten," she said. She didn't persuade me. She simply let me know the cold-water facts. Then she asked me what I wanted to do. It was the first chance I had ever had to answer that question, and I told and told—about Mr. Drew who was supposed to teach me elocution to get rid of a speech impediment but instead introduced me to Shakespeare, with whom I had well and truly fallen in love, as I was in love with Katharine Hepburn, and I wanted with my whole heart and talent to be a classical actress, and on and on. My story was, I am sure now, strongly imitative of Katharine in *Morning Glory*, which for me at seventeen had replaced the King James Bible. All that I had stored up within my own silence in the magic darkness of the place where movie met dream I poured out to Kaye Brown. She did not stop me.

That blessed woman heard me out as if she hadn't heard the story from every fledgling actress before. I finished, realized what I had done, and sat frozen. She began to ask very practical questions. If my father would pay for lessons. If I had to earn a living. Where I was staying. As I look back now, I see that it was a miraculous action when she could have simply shut me up, declared the interview over, and politely thrown me out of her office. I was so lucky.

There was one other who was an angel in disguise when I could have been, and later was, ripped apart. His name was Johnny Kennerly. He was the casting director for the Shuberts, and his office was a Mecca and a retreat for the young, the hopeful, and anybody else who managed to find him.

Johnny Kennerly had been a female impersonator until the puritans swooped down and made what he did illegal. That is all I ever knew about him—that and the welcome he gave in a dreary round that I made every morning because that was what you did. I sat with the other unemployed and waited until a harried secretary shouted, "No casting." I wonder if it is the same now. Never changing. The parade of the hopeful that turns after a time into the parade of the disappointed, and the job as a waiter is taken, or the offer from "out of town," it doesn't matter where; the address is always "out of town."

Johnny Kennerly's office was completely different. It was a visit, and you were welcomed as if he had invited you. He actually took the trouble to learn names. When I asked him once why he did it, he said, "I've been there."

So almost every morning that fall, I went through the magic lobby of the Shubert Theater, where posters for famous shows from the twenties hung along the walls. Once I shared the elevator with Harpo Marx. He was a small, shy man wearing a homburg and a black overcoat, like a hundred other men you passed in those streets in that part of New York in 1938 without noticing them. I only knew who it was when we went in the same door.

One morning I got my "big break." It was in the late fall, I remember, because it was very cold and the wind came tearing through Forty-second Street from the East River. I wore the black skunk coat my mother had thought correct for a northern winter. Johnny Kennerly had warned me that I dressed too well, that I didn't look as if I needed a job. I said they were all the clothes I had.

There were five or six people in the room. A tall man with black hair stood by Johnny Kennerly's desk, watching the door. When I went in, he said, "Will you read for me? I'm casting for a new summer theater." Johnny introduced us and we went into one of the small rooms off the main office. I don't remember what I read, partly because the reaction to the reading was so powerful it blotted out any other recall.

The man jumped up and ran into the outer office. He shouted, "She's a natural. She's a natural." It caused the people in the room to move, get up, and settle back down as if a strong wind had blown through the room. Johnny Kennerly was as delighted as if I were his baby.

The man's name was William Castle. Later, in Hollywood, he was to make horror films. When we went back into the little room (all this banality is important, burned on my brain), he said, "You are my discovery. You will be my lead next summer. What I want you to do is this. Get out of New York and go home, wherever that is. Come back on the first of May. I don't want anybody else to see you."

I was, of course, ecstatic. I called my family. They were as delighted as I was, principally because it meant my coming home. Somehow that underlay every decision. My father promised to send me back for the first of May. It became, for me, as important as it might have been to witches in the thirteenth century, or Communists in the nineteenth and twentieth.

I studied hard at home and the new house grew. I had voice lessons, which I still remember: I am standing beside a piano trilling scales. My father paid for that, and for more dancing lessons, although he insisted that it be ballroom dancing. I was relieved. I had never been any good at Miss Embleton's tap and ballet classes, which I had trudged to, knowing failure, twice a week since I was nine. In one recital, Miss Embleton hadn't known what to do with me, but she knew I wrote poetry, à la James Whitcomb Riley. So I dressed up as a little old lady and recited my poem about a burglar.

When the recital was over, all the parents went back and hugged their children and told them how good they were—the ones who had fallen down, the ones who had forgotten their steps, all of them. My mother walked in, grabbed my hand so hard it hurt, and marched me out. She sounded furious: "Don't you *ever* humiliate me like that again."

But that time between Thanksgiving of 1938 and the first of May 1939 was entirely happy, for me and for my parents. The house was growing into the first Queen Anne house on South Hills. And we were all involved in a perpetual crossing of the lace bridge—every morning driving upward into the hills, then down again at night to our rented rooms.

Around the new house, my father and I planted shrubs that he had dug up in the mountains.

I even had the nerve to beard the most frightening man I knew. It was Judge G. W. McClintic, who was rumored to have lost all his friends when he became a judge during Prohibition and jailed his friends' bootleggers.

I saw him on his porch, sitting in his swing. I had to go up the steps, yearning for nepotism. He was Guthrie McClintic's uncle to me, and I didn't know any bootleggers. Guthrie McClintic was the foremost director of the classics in New York. His wife was Katharine Cornell, who had played Juliet in the first Shakespearean play I had ever seen in New York. I had thought she was too old and it made me cry. But after that, I had seen her as Mrs. Alving in Ibsen's *Ghosts*, and as Elizabeth

Barrett Browning to Brian Aherne's Robert Browning in *The Barretts of Wimpole Street*. The only line of that I still remember is, "When I wrote that, God and Robert Browning knew what it meant. Now only God knows."

All of that pushed me up the porch steps to stumble and introduce myself to the judge.

He looked at me: "I bet you don't even know who your grandfather was." I heard his voice as, of course, savage. I was able, just, to tell him who both grandfathers were.

He began to smile. It was very slow. He told me to sit down beside him, and we began to swing, just barely, like we had been sitting there for a long time.

I could not say a word, but he could. He said, "I bet you want to be an actress."

Want! What a small word for so great a destiny. I was sure of that if of nothing else in the world. I must have been looking at the painted arm of the swing, for I remember it, when I heard him say, "Why don't I write to my nephew and introduce you? He probably won't promise anything, but he will see you."

Whatever came after that is blank. But I do remember that he told me to stop by again when he was sitting on his porch. How did he know? It is only now, as I remember, that I wonder if my mother had called him. She was so capable of a kindness like that, and also of not telling me.

So, full of health and training and joy, I went back to New York. I walked into Johnny Kennerly's office. A friend who was also a refugee from Sweet Briar was sitting on the corner of his desk. She wore a lavender turban wrapped around her hair. I still don't know why I knew something was wrong when I saw her; she actually hugged me.

William Castle turned up a long hour later. He looked at

me for a long time and then said, "I'm sorry, but I won't be able to use you this summer. Maybe later."

I left the office and rode down in the elevator that had been such a wonderful ride to hope and glory. I stood on Forty-second Street, literally not knowing which way to go.

My fellow Sweet Briar refugee came out of the building. "He said you had lost that dramatic quality he wanted. He said you looked bucolic." I will never forget the word. "He said you looked too happy."

It took a week for me to find the guts to call my parents. My father told me to come home at once. I told them I had signed on with the John Robert Powers modeling agency. My father blew up.

"I would rather have my daughter a whore than a model," he yelled, which he seldom did.

The guts sustained my answer. "It doesn't pay as much," I told them. I hear a remark in my mother's voice but not what she said.

I was standing in the nearest phone booth to the Powers agency. I could see the door where the models walked in and out in their high heels and black dresses, looking, that year, older than they were, with their hats tipped over one eye. They carried black hat boxes that told the world they had been chosen to do what I was to find that summer to be the hardest work I have ever done.

Because I had a mass of curling auburn hair, most of the few jobs I got were color shots where I sat under hot klieg lights in heavy pancake makeup, not daring to move a muscle or even sigh, while the photographer talked on the phone.

I moved to the newer Harry Conover Agency, where other models had gone. Powers was so large that if you were new and less known, there was too much competition. Besides, at Harry Conover, I was paid ten dollars an hour instead of the five with which I had started.

Then, in midsummer, I took a job on Seventh Avenue, at the Traina wholesale showroom. All day long I worked in a circular assembly line. Half of the circle was inside the dressing room, the other half outside, in the showroom. In the dressing room, I would pull off the dress I had just modeled, put on the next one, touch my hair, wet my lips, and hurry to the door of the showroom. There I would step out, slowly, slowly, in the slightly bored saunter that was fashionable that summer, pausing from time to time and freezing into the right pose with my pelvis slightly forward, in what was known as the Venus curve. I had been instructed to stop in front of buyers from Texas and any other rich states where women could afford Traina's very expensive clothes.

Those few weeks branded me with a love of fine clothes. The fall of dresses of the cloth that cost, even then, and even wholesale, up to three hundred dollars in pre–World War II money, a sum that was keeping me in New York and paying for my classical lessons in Shakespearean heroines for a month.

Oh, but the cloth felt wonderful against my skin.

For the rest, during that five or six weeks, I carried a large purse as body armor against the riot of boys pushing long-wheeled trolleys with dresses swinging from their hangers, who had a joking way of pinching our breasts if we passed too near. Dodging the hangers, the trucks, the nameless crowds that patrolled Times Square, I found an Automat for my lunch.

The showroom was air-conditioned. The dressing room was not. All day we passed from heat to cold, cold to heat. In the whole time I was there, only one person ever looked up at my face. I was a coat hanger who could walk. After we had circled languidly through the showroom and back into the dressing room, we were suddenly frantic, with only a minute or two to change, hang up clothes, and rush to the door again, where we walked languidly around the showroom, over and over, all day long. One afternoon I fainted from the heat. The only comment was, "When you feel faint, take off the model clothes."

I quit.

In the evening, from May onward, I lived in the last truly elegant season that ever would be in New York—a season of the World's Fair, the St. Regis Roof, the Stork Club, the 21 Club, interiors by Billy Baldwin, Fray and Braggiotti at the piano, Django Reinhardt, cars with leather seats, and thousands of Europeans. In the daytime, I did the rounds of the theatrical agents, then reported to the modeling agency. I stood or leaned like a frozen thing under the klieg lights.

I had three entirely separate groups of friends. One included Vernon Duke, the composer/songwriter who liked to hole up in the Carlyle Hotel with very fat women when he finished a piece of work; Constantin Alajalov, who painted covers for *The New Yorker*; and Jacques Fray and Mario Braggiotti, a piano duo. Then there was a group of young English men who were having what they feared was a last summer in New York, working. The last were friends, most of whom worked for Henry Luce at *Time*; we met in a bar that we made into a kind of club on, I think, Forty-eighth Street.

It was the summer of the World's Fair, and we all knew—those of us who thought at all—that it was the last time. We didn't talk about it. We danced the rumba, and joined the conga lines, and tried to look sophisticated and bored because that was the fashion. I think an imitation of the fashion is back. I saw a young girl in New York last winter lounging in a yawn and a black satin evening dress at one of those never-ending charity balls. It reminded me of how I had tried so hard to look bored, too, when inside I was as excited as a child, the child I was. It also reminded me of a caption on a Thurber cartoon, "She tries to look enigmatic, but she only succeeds in looking sleepy."

2

THE LAST GRAND SUMMER

❧

New York City is quieter now. The Klaxons calling from the East River are gone. In the summer of 1939, they were almost hourly announcements that New York was a seaport, allied by ocean to the world. From wherever we were in midtown Manhattan, we heard the bovine hoots of the ships leaving their docks in the East River from a hundred piers.

They sailed in and out of the harbor as if, unspoken and unadmitted, it was their last chance. The atmosphere, the conversation, the plans for the day became more important. We demanded that the last twilight before war be daylight still, as if we were children who thought they could wish it so.

There were days in July when the flow from the docks into Manhattan seemed unending, as far inland as Times Square, where I was, so much of the time, earning a living of sorts. I thought myself more independent than I was. My father didn't abandon me altogether. It would have been against his whole view of himself as caretaker for his family, and he was honestly and rightly worried. But he did insist that I cash checks at the 21 Club. He said he trusted it because it was a club. I did not point out, ever, that it had been the most famous speakeasy in New York. In the summer of 1939, with its hierarchy of tables, political and famous, the 21 Club was where successful, would-be-successful, infamous, and those special men whom Roosevelt had appointed as "dollar a year" men were to be seen.

At the bar, those who were waiting to be noticed, and those who would be noticed, waited. One evening, when I got there early for a dinner date, I talked with the young actor Orson Welles. I told him I had seen him as Tybalt, and made it sound like a compliment; I didn't say I had hated it.

The days were bright with sun, and the nights, bright with city lights, but the fashionable colors that summer were black and white, Billy Baldwin and Chanel. From the theater district to Central Park, men dressed in black tie, and the taxis had leather seats, and everybody smoked and drank like Nick and Nora.

Union Square was filled with people trying to pick up news of the slaughter of the Spanish Civil War. Men from the *Herald Tribune* in soft brimmed hats and raincoats ranged from the Algonquin Hotel south to Union Square, where people traded news and rumors about the debacle. Everybody was preoccupied, and trying not to be; maybe that was why we concentrated on pleasure, like people on leave from a war that hadn't yet happened.

In a studio in the Village, I learned Shakespeare's heroines from a teacher whose name I have forgotten. But on my own, I read the plays aloud and would cry—even though they were so familiar—when Sir John Falstaff babbled of green fields, and Hamlet and Richard II had, for me, the voice of Maurice Evans.

The World's Fair, from the Great White Way—where the rides and the freaks and the Aquacade were—to the grand temples to American industry, promised a future no one believed in. The buildings were, in the words and fashion of the time, streamlined. Their exteriors were softened into graceful curves as if they were in a high wind, taking off into some promised land, and those of us who knew it wasn't true tended to huddle together.

The interiors of those temporary buildings that looked so solid were in constant movement—mechanical marching of cows and railroads, cars and electronic promises, pioneers and robots and tumbles, falls, veils of water rushed toward that overused, ephemeral tomorrow. And we knew it; we all knew it.

The grandest and most elegant were the pavilions of France, Great Britain, and Italy, with their flags, their advertised dignified taste, and their restaurants, which had become fashionable as soon as they were opened. From a window in the restaurant of the French Pavilion, I watched the tiny, doll-like figures of the king and queen of England far below, followed by an enormous crowd around a formal lake called the Lagoon of Nations.

The lined-up industrial promises, the countries of Europe in architectural triumphs of the late thirties looked blond, as if the best-known architects in the world, who had been hired to design them, were one creative mind seeing visions of movement and promise, all in that last summer.

Glass glittered in the sun by day and the manmade stars by night, and water caught all the light and color in flung jets, falls, and fans. Alexander Calder's wonderful veil of water was more magical than its name, the Water Ballet. Fluorescent forms of light showed the way along wide walking streets. On a tower above the Italian Pavilion, the great goddess Roma sat above the crowds. The USSR building was, that year, the most popular national building at the fair. Higher than Roma—or so it seemed—was a handsome statue of a healthy worker, whose arm held high the red star.

A sea of people strolled along the wide parades, where statues of anatomically impossible high-breasted, strong-muscled women with huge thighs, and square-cut marble men, represented the view of the human body in 1939. If any of us who were earning a living modeling that year had sported such massive legs and thighs, we would have been fired.

Over it all loomed as simple a design as ever caught the imagination, the Trylon and the Perisphere. They dominated the fair, magnificently still.

Everybody had a job, and it was all as temporary as a circus. The fair advertised the immortality of national borders and big business. My Sweet Briar friend who had informed me about how I lost my first acting job was a disembodied head in one of the sideshows.

At the top of the tower for the parachute jump, the most popular ride at the fair, I sat, terrified and stunned with the vision of the fair below, in a small chair high in the night sky, in the inevitable evening dress. The tall steel tower looked as frail as lace. For a minute before release, I looked down at the Trylon and the Perisphere and the sea bottom of lights far below. The chair was released; the following two or three seconds of free fall still affect my dreams of lost, dark, terrifying, wonderful freedom. I floated above the fair lights, it seemed, forever. I felt the jerk of the parachute opening, and then I floated down into the light where Flushing Meadows had been turned into that summer's miracle.

In mid-July, three cruisers from the French navy moored at Pier 100 on a goodwill cruise, with newly graduated officers from Saint-Cyr, the French Naval Academy. They docked across the pier from the ocean liner *Normandie*, that year the most gloriously grand and golden ship in the world. She had been made into the flagship of the French navy for the goodwill visit to New York.

Those of us who had connections—and I have no idea now what mine were, maybe friends from Sweet Briar—received embossed invitations to a champagne reception aboard the *Normandie*. It was that summer's invitation to kill for. There was much telephoning to and fro about protocol. Did you turn the upper right side or the upper left side of your calling card to accept, or did you turn one of the bottom corners of your calling card to regret? Or did you have calling cards in the first place? I ordered them at a stationer's on Third Avenue. I remember trying to find a twenty-four-hour service—making a sprint across Madison and Park Avenues from a house near a corner of Madison Avenue in the East Sixties, which was the usual brownstone outside and a boardinghouse within. One of the models had persuaded me I needed a "better address." My fellow inmates were there for the same reasons.

The day of the reception, I walked slowly along the pier in the sun by the huge *Normandie*. Slowly not for dignity but so that I wouldn't perspire in my best green linen, my high heels, my white gloves, my silk stockings, my garter belt, my white silk slip, my white step-ins; I had had drummed into my soul that any other color of underwear would condemn me as "one of them" if I were in a wreck. I did not cover with a hat the crowning glory of my healthy, waving, auburn hair, suitably touched and moved by a slight summer breeze from the sea.

That year we all tried to look older than we were, because the perfect woman of 1939 was thirty-five years old, very chic, formed by Chanel and with a nod to Mrs. Simpson, who had married the Prince of Wales, who had become the Duke of Windsor and had been shunted off to be governor of Bermuda to get him out of the limelight. It hadn't worked. They seemed to be on one official visit to New York after another, often photographed at El Morocco.

So a long line of snobberies went tripping along the pier to where young sailors waited to hand us onto the awning-covered gangplank.

The stairs curved in a magnificent arc. The whole room, the sunlight, the walls, the glass seemed touched with gold. It was the grandest room I had ever seen. At the foot of the wide, Hollywood-style entrance, an admiral of the French fleet stood with a small notebook and a gold pencil in his hands. I saw him give a barely perceptible nod to the sailor who was escorting me, I suppose so I wouldn't crash down the stairs at his feet out of sheer wonder. I was guided toward him. He asked my name, my address. One day later, another embossed invitation arrived at the boardinghouse with the good address. It was an invitation to the Bastille Day ball aboard the twin cruisers *Georges Leygues* and *Montcalm*.

They had been lashed together so that a dance floor covered the two decks amidships. A champagne bar had replaced the forward gun.

At a few minutes to midnight, the band stopped and everybody stood waiting. Behind me was Maury Paul, known as Cholly Knickerbocker or "Champagne Cholly," the gossip columnist for the Hearst papers, whose main claim to fame had been his coining of the phrase *café society*.

He whispered in my ear, "Mary Lee, you are standing next to the third pretender to the French throne!"

At 12:01 on July 14, the guns on the French cruiser *Gloire* boomed out over the harbor to herald Bastille Day.

"What French throne?" I whispered back to him.

How I knew him or he knew me I have no idea now. It was all part of that spring and summer of 1939. And how, the next day, I went to the World's Fair with a new lieutenant in the French navy named Philippe Lann from the

Georges Leygues, and another who came from Lyon, I don't remember either.

I only see us on the subway going out to the fair, and I see glimpses of us strolling around that day among the bright flashing waterfalls and white buildings in Flushing Meadows, talking about the war that was a shadow over both of us in that bright sun. In his bad English and my bad French, we two, both twenty, talked all day.

I wondered for years whether Philippe Lann had been killed when the French fleet was scuttled at Oran. Then I found on the Internet that the *Georges Leygues* and the *Montcalm* had been in harbor at Dakar in West Africa when the French surrendered. They had both joined the Free French under Charles de Gaulle, stationed in England. The *Georges Leygues* had been in the D-Day landing.

I look back on so many different lives that summer with my friends who were so apart from each other, and I ask why about all of them, for the connections are gone. Why was I on Gardiner's Island for lunch on a Sunday with a young man they were all making fun of? I met Alfred de Liagre, whom I saw many times later, but I remember most a man introduced as a white hunter, whose name was Bror Blixen. Because I knew later that he was married to that wonderful woman Karen Blixen, who wrote *Out of Africa* and the magic short stories as Isak Dinesen.

But the most astonishing time, later in the summer, was a modeling job I received because I could shoot.

⁓

I have known so many of the lost ships and their ritual sailings—the two *Queens, Mary and Elizabeth*; the lovely *Britannic*, flagship of the old White Star Line; the *Conte de Savoie*; the *Mauretania*; the *Ile de France* as a luxury hotel and a troop ship; and even the *City of Benares*, built for the voyages to and from India. But they sailed in other times to other places. I was to cross the Atlantic eleven times in the next twelve years. Only one of those ships sailed in the summer of 1939—the *Conte de Savoie*, on a weekend cruise to Bermuda.

What do I remember of the first ship? It seemed to be a hotel surrounded by the sea. I began, as soon as we were out of sight of land, to feel confined. I knew nobody. The other models all seemed to be friends; in a little time, I began to realize that it was a way of being together, whether or not they had ever seen each other before—part of the job we had been hired to do.

We were being paid to be friends, and then, humans being what they are, we began to slip into true ease with each other. It was, I realized, my first professional acting job. I was cast as a skeet shooter. The only gun I had ever shot was a rifle. Nobody on the advertising "shoot" knew the difference or cared. I was to smile, be at ease, lounge gracefully—a professional little community imitating affection as we were imitating true travelers, sitting at professional ease. Seeming to converse. Seeming to travel.

Around us, the true travelers we were imitating faded out of our attention. We were a separate breed, all strangers to me and, I realized later, to each other, but the others knew how to form that professional group. I didn't. A beautiful woman, known as Pretty Anita Colby, took me in hand. I have been grateful to her ever since. In those days, it was impossible to air-brush color photographs, so, because of my freckles, I was of little use except at the skeet balcony that thrust out from the first-class deck—over the water nearly three stories below.

The first time I fired the shotgun, it nearly knocked me

down. We began work as soon as we were at sea. The sun was hot, the makeup had to be patted and renewed; so much of the photographing required standing around, waiting, posing, smiling, and waiting again. I collected across my nose the freckles that are the price I paid for the rich crop of auburn hair that had made the photographers hire me that summer. I had not only a sprinkle of freckles but also a black bruise the size of a fifty-cent coin on the soft place at my shoulder where I had been taught by a nice young camp counselor from Princeton to nestle a gun. After the pictures in the shooting cage, I was only photographed with my back to the camera. On deck, at the swimming pool, in the bar (evening clothes in the daytime while the regular passengers were at lunch), we were languid. It was like any other modeling job, only there was a pitch to the deck, and a sea that interfered.

We were given the day off in Bermuda—from docking in the morning to the early evening. We went to the shops in a huddle with the other tourists and bought perfume. From the deck rail, I watched the sea at sunset. The huge orb, now a radiant orange, began to flatten as if it were being forced down into the water of the horizon, and slowly the whole sky streamed red.

There is a first time for things. That time of change, from sunset into twilight at sea, has called me through the years every time that it was not storming. Whether I was watching the softer sun of the North Atlantic or the cold sun of winter, it was as if I had an appointment I could not miss whenever I was at sea.

The *Conte de Savoie* sailed out of the harbor in Bermuda at the beginning of summer twilight. In a short time, unnoticed, we were out of sight of land. The last photographing session was over. We had drinks and dinner, I suppose. I remember none of this happening, only the fact that it did.

But after dinner, in the lounge bar with its wide, soft, thirties-style comfortable chairs around a large table, it is as if I sit there still. I think we forgot for the evening that we were not part of the weekend cruise of the people around us, who, imitating us, had made shipboard friendships. There were pools of laughter. Two, then three couples got up to dance to the Italian band that played dance music with the bored beat of musicians who had played the same music too many times.

We had been sitting in the same lounge seats where we had been photographed, as if we had laid claim to them, and what begins for me now is more than memory. It is a reliving. The others had fallen into telling dirty jokes as if they were hiding the fact that they were protecting themselves from conversation. Quietness, a pause, had triumphed over the band and the empty laughter.

When I got up to leave, I thought nobody noticed. I was withdrawing from the evening duties of comradely pleasure, forced and exhausting. There was no passion in this, no conscious decision. It was simply, I see now, a turning away. I think now that I simply wanted the sea air instead of the scents of cigarettes and perfume. I did not yet know I was changing course.

I walked out of the soft yellow light of the room with its subtlety of lamps. The first clean darkness of the deck ignored the discrete lights that cast shadows of the empty deck chairs and lit the doors to the long corridors leading to the cabins. I walked around the deck, aware of being afloat on the huge sea in a boat—not a hotel, not a bar, not a luxurious ship with its thirties taupe-and-tan soft upholstery and the same oversimple, fashionable, marble-and-chrome bodies as the World's Fair.

At sea, really at sea, for the first time at home in it, I stopped and leaned my arms on the rail and rested there, three stories above the water. Below me, the lights from the portholes and the lower decks made a plan of the ship in the dark ocean. I don't know how long I had been there when I first saw them, or they saw me.

There were two of them, not gay and happy in any terms I knew but so simply there, at home in the sea. They were neither seductive nor frightening. They were just there, at the ocean surface, watching the ship. A man and a woman had leaped up above the water surface, to their waists; her hair was long, his shorter. They steadied each other with their arms across each other's backs. They waved. They were in their element, I in mine. They were not waving to draw my attention. I knew that. I have no idea how. They waved as part of the leap, a reaching out, playful. They were pale, as pale as white mist.

They did not draw me toward them, nor did I try to get their attention. I had a sense that we were glimpsing each other in passing and should not disturb each other. Gradually, across the water's surface, I saw more figures, some gamboling high enough for me to see their upper bodies, and some, in my terms, weaker, their faces profiles in the water, as if they had not the strength or wish to rise into the air. I watched until they began to fade, hundreds of them all the way beyond my sight. I was not frightened or excited; I was completely at peace.

Someone came up beside me. It was one of the photographers. He said, "You've been out here for three hours. We wondered if you were all right. I knocked on the door of your cabin. You weren't there. What are you doing out here?" I did not answer his question. I simply pointed at the fading figures. "Look."

He yelled, "Holy Mary Mother of God," and pulled me away from the rail. "Get away from here. Get away."

Six years later, I was walking along Madison Avenue behind St. Patrick's Cathedral when I saw two men coming toward me. One of them was the photographer. His name was O'Reilly. He had begun his career during the Depression with a risky feat in order to establish himself as a professional photographer. In 1931, he had climbed the steel rigging of the unfinished Empire State Building and had taken the first pictures of New York from its highest point. There were still, in the late thirties, too many ghosts from a desperate time when courage was not a choice. It was survival. I have wondered since then if all the talk of the generation's bravery, and the civilian's nonsense about "heroes," was the unrecognized training of Depression children.

He saw me and laughed. As they stopped to say hello, he said to the other man, "Watch out for that woman. She makes you see things."

3

WAITING

❦

I did not do it consciously, the change of course. But I did
know that the importance of things was changing. I have to
look back to see how. I was not aware even of choice. I only
know that I gave up modeling—not as a gesture, as I would do
later. I simply no longer went to the modeling agency.

I spent my time with people who were not ignoring "the
gathering storm" but watching the horizon. Stephen Spender's
line, "We who live under the shadow of a war, what can we do
that matters?" seemed the whining of children or dancers, or
the crowds that gathered ignoring the fact that it was already
beginning to rain.

I was an American in a group of Europeans of conscription
age, a polyglot group whose drawing together, like my joining
them, was an unrealized huddle for some protection. From
change? From danger? From the end of something we had not
cared for in the first place? I only remember that we drew
together and made quick friendships.

Several of them were English. One became my closest
friend, like a shipboard romance made too quickly, as if there
were no time to try to know each other. He had the wonderful

41

English name of Rodney Douglas De Vaughan Weathersbee. He was working at J. Walter Thompson as an intern for the summer before going to the business school chosen by his father in the fall. There was no weighing of talent, merit, or social position with any of the group. We were simply together, watching—sometimes from walks in Central Park, sometimes in one-room apartments in the East Thirties, and often, since it was larger and the parents welcomed us, in the heavy Eastern European elegance of an apartment on Fifth Avenue. They were belligerently White Russians. The father was a Russian count, and he had brought out of Russia two large, horse-drawn carts with enough works of art to set up a thriving business in New York.

It did not seem odd at the time, only now as I remember it for the first time in years, that such a new and more stringent life would begin in the greatest luxury I had ever seen. Because it was so integrated into their lives, I took it for granted. That was the way they were, or still were, the last of the tsarist Russians to live in full glory and vast debt in New York.

The younger son, Nicky, was Rodney's friend. Our birthdays were a month apart. His twenty-first birthday was celebrated in the best Russian lost glory.

I was asked to dinner. It was incredible even for the New York of the last days of true luxury. The table linen was heavily embroidered with the family crest. The silver was not silver but gold. The wine glasses were a foot high. At one end of the table the father sat; at the other, an old friend, an officer in the Imperial Guard. Nicky's fiancée was there, as well as his older brother, his mother, Rodney, and, at the far end of the table, the officer in the Imperial Guard. I had not yet read *War and Peace*, but I knew that for an evening I was living it.

The dessert was a decorated ice-cream tower that had been flown from Paris. It was brought to the table to be admired and then taken back to the kitchen to be cut and served. New glasses were filled with champagne. It was the father, not the mother, who took the first bite, and we all began to eat it. My gold spoon bent like a pretzel. I spent the first few minutes of dessert trying to bend it back into shape, wrapped in my napkin in my lap, hoping no one would notice.

We had drunk wine and then champagne, and then, after the dessert, the count brought out a bottle of brandy that he explained had been put down at Nicky's birth. Since he was my age, that was 1918. Even I, ignorant as I was, knew that the Russian Revolution was in full terror then. I wondered what this man might have been up to, to move such luxury out of Russia in that year. He nestled the bottle in his arm as if it were the newborn baby. It would have been rude to question, and in that room, rudeness would have been unthinkable.

Small brandy glasses were placed in front of him. He made a speech about Nicky and his birthday; toward the end of it, he lapsed into Russian. Then he poured the brandy. I was sitting on his left and realized that there were not enough glasses. He poured carefully, and we all watched the golden brown brandy catch the candlelight. He handed a glass to Nicky, one to Rodney, one to the Imperial Guard officer, one to himself, and one to me. I was the only woman at the table chosen for the toast. Obviously, I thought it was because I was an American. Nicky's fiancée was already considered to be of the Russian family; Russian women obviously did not drink brandy, not at that table.

The room smelled of brandy, candle wax, and flowers. The ritual went slowly on. None of us looked at each other. He walked around the table and handed the bottle and an empty glass to the officer, who stood to receive it. The host went back to his place at the head of the table.

The officer filled his glass to the brim. He toasted Nicky and refilled his glass. He toasted the mother, who sat beside him; he toasted the host; and he toasted Nicky's fiancée. Each time he filled his glass. We were all taking little burning sips, but by the time he had finished his toasting, our glasses were empty and the bottle was only a quarter full. Then he sat down. The host was drunk or stunned. He sat there, looking like the bust of Beethoven, staring at something none of us, I'm sure, could see.

The women went into the living room, where we had coffee and little to say to each other. Nicky's mother spoke little English. She had been left adrift with strangers. It was a formal drawing room, the same room where later we all waited for the whole weekend after the invasion by Hitler of Poland, sleeping and waking, watched by large eighteenth-century Russian portraits that Nicky and his brother made fun of when their parents weren't around.

In the month of August, I went to my acting lessons in Shakespeare. Guthrie McClintic called me into his office and told me he was casting me as the younger sister in Katharine Cornell's *Major Barbara*. At any time before the onrush of a future we knew was coming and did not name yet, I would have been in midair. I kept thinking that I should be more ecstatic than I was. After all, the wish I had carried within me for years was coming true. A week later, he called to say they had decided to cancel the play because they had found out that Wendy Hiller was making a film of *Major Barbara*. I remember wondering who she was. The whole incident was more a preoccupation than a disaster.

That weekend, beginning on Friday morning with the news

that Hitler had gone into Poland, was, for me, one of those times of disaster when you remember where you were, how you heard, what you were doing, the scene around you, the trees, a flag being lowered to half-mast. The news flashes from the Polish government that the Polish cavalry was standing up to the blitzkrieg were pathetic. What was beginning to happen had nothing to do with raw courage, and we knew it.

The center of life was in that Russian apartment that we had made into a waiting place when Hitler made his move. Nicky's parents were not there. I have no idea now where they were. We messed up the kitchen and drank wine from the count's cellar, which wasn't a cellar but a cupboard in the hall.

The news came before dawn; we had been awake all night. Then the days began to stretch into more than days and nights, a single waiting time, when the people around me, the men—boys really, I know now—began to talk of going back. Joining up. Joining up. It was the first time I had ever heard that strange phrase. Not *joining*. Joining up. Several of them, including Rodney, were planning to go to Canada to join the Canadian army or air force. The whole direction was toward an announcement that did not seem ever to be coming. I remember one saying that if England didn't go to war this time, he was going to become an American out of shame. Another agreed with him. War was already in that room. We talked of the Spanish war that was being lost; we talked of Austria, and the white socks worn by gentlemen there to show they were Nazis. And the Rhineland, and Czechoslovakia, and all the land that had fallen to Hitler while nobody did anything to stop him. And the fact that not only had the democracies allowed Franco to win in Spain with the aid of Germany and Italy but also had thrown the elected republic into the hands of a minority left-wing party, the Communists.

War—not yet The War—was taking our lives. I see us all now as young and growing older by the hour, boys who no longer for me have names, figures in that room, arguing, sleeping, eating, drinking, waiting, through Friday, through Saturday. During an argument, somebody threw scrambled eggs, which made an extra ruffle on a painted skirt of some dead Russian aristocrat.

I remember going back to my room at the boardinghouse with the good address to change clothes. I have looked for that house, somewhere in the East Sixties, since then. But I don't recognize it. It is lost to me among the remaining brownstones with their impersonal façades.

A young German friend who lived in the building knocked on my door. He was so upset that I offered to take a walk with him. It must have already been evening; I remember darkness and the lights of Central Park when we walked there. It was normal, and for us so abnormal, the cars passing, the horse-drawn carriages with their couples in evening clothes, lots of them. It was a fashion that summer. Rodney and I had ridden in a carriage in the park a week earlier. We were in evening clothes, and, quite awkwardly, he asked me to marry him.

I didn't answer, not that night.

My German friend and I walked deep into the park while he cursed Hitler, the nasty little upstart corporal, as if he had been thrust back into the first days of the takeover of Napoleon, a French instead of a German aristocrat. His family, who lived on Park Avenue, had come to New York to get him out of the clutches of Hitler. Living in the boardinghouse was, for him, a step into maturity. He said that. He was a very serious young man. He told me that night how he had joined the Hitler Youth like all of the other boys in his class, and how they had marched through Berlin chanting, "Anyone who doesn't vote for Hitler goes to Dachau." It was the first time I heard and remembered the name of a concentration camp. Anyone who says we did not know what was going on then is lying either to themselves or to others. We knew. It was all around us. We stumbled on it in conversations. We heard stories. A dear friend, Carol Rothschild, told me that their apartment was so full of relatives that the babies slept in dresser drawers. Another, who had been to school in Switzerland, told me that her best friend, a German girl, had been made to scrub the street on her knees while people jeered.

I have never remembered names well, but I still see his face and hear his voice, the heavy accent. Once he cried. We walked for three hours, until the cars and the carriages had long since left the park. This was not a courageous or foolish decision. Nobody feared Central Park then. I had often walked in company after an evening at the Stork Club in that mixture of the profound and the foolish that was New York in the summer of 1939.

The last thing my German friend said was, "I will have to go back, of course." When I asked why, after what he had told me, he said, "My country will be at war."

So many lights had been turned out when we walked back to the boardinghouse that we remarked on being able to see the stars.

When I got back to the Russians' apartment, the sky above the building opposite was growing gray, the only sign of dawn in the cavernous street below. Some were asleep, some still drinking. Rodney hardly registered that I had been away. We waited; sometimes we talked, sometimes we slept, arguments over, opinions already delivered.

"It's out of our hands now," somebody said, and it sounded so ominous I was afraid of crying at that mundane cliché.

We seemed to be the only people in the city who were awake and waiting. Someone kept leaning his head closer to the ever-fading signal from the radio. He called out, "Quiet!" louder than he needed to. I think I remember the toll of bells, very faint. The tin voice from very far away began, "I am speaking to you from the cabinet room at Ten Downing Street." The room was dead quiet.

I remember that, and then a blank of memory and then, either fading back in or I realized what was said—"How tired his voice sounds," I remember thinking that—the thin, wavy voice of a dog-tired old man. It was Neville Chamberlain, who had promised "peace in our time." What else he said I have forgotten, but not the words, "Consequently, this country is at war with Germany."

The room seemed to explode around me, and the voice went on like a faint echo behind us in the background. But nobody listened.

We were not aware yet that everything we took for granted was disappearing or changing, like a shaken kaleidoscope, not of colors but of time and sound and habit and decision.

We thought later, as we got used to the fact, that we, if nobody else we passed in the New York street knew it, were at war, a conscious war. It was many years before I knew from his poem, "September 1, 1939," that W. H. Auden had sat in a bar across town, thinking the same thing.

The unconscious war had been going on since 1936, ever since Hitler's election was recognized for what it was. Every time he colonized another small country in Europe, there was the awareness that it had to happen sometime. At first the voices had been whispers. There were passionate arguments. I remember saying one night during an argument that I was a future Gold Star Mother. Being for or against stopping Hitler was a fashion that we honestly thought was a matter of individual decision.

It all changed so profoundly, so deeply, in that moment that Neville Chamberlain finally spoke, that we thought the French phrase was right—"The more things change, the more they remain the same." How wrong that was.

Rodney and I thought we were deciding to be married. We were simply being swept along by change and needed to cling to each other like people in a flood. We kept planning in order to find some known and safe simplicity instead of what was facing all of us. I had been twenty-one for a month, and Rodney was twenty-three. We were enveloped in our romantic vision of a safe affection. We were, as we were supposed to be, "in love" with each other. We shared a terrible fear of being alone in what was coming.

On a weekday morning, we went down to a part of New York neither of us had ever seen, to City Hall. The only thing I remember is standing in a long, long line of quiet couples, maybe like us, flogged into action by the news, maybe just New Yorkers who made long lines to be married every day. Much of the rest of the week is blank. I know what happened, but I do not see it happening. The memory is as intellectual as if I had read about that first week of war in a book. The only thing I see again is Rodney's hand reaching forward to a piece of paper. It is our marriage license.

We knew that Rodney would go to war within days, that London was going to be obliterated just as Warsaw was now being leveled. We were guided in our decision by the vast current of our own visceral reactions to war, by radio voices describing the running crowds, the pathetically brave Polish cavalry decimated by the tanks of Hitler's blitzkrieg—the new word that was becoming familiar—by panic and death in strange streets. Our ambitions—his to be a writer, mine to be an actress—diminished into dreams.

One thing we learned at once. It was to be the most important talent in wartime. How to wait. Nothing happened at once. After the first air-raid warning that Sunday morning in London, nothing happened there. In New York, we rented a furnished apartment by the week; we thought we would be leaving for Canada almost at once.[1] I remember its door, its darkness, the way gray light came in the window before I cleaned it. By incessant scrubbing, I tried to get rid of a long line of unknown slobs.

We were bombarded not by bombs but by decisions that seemed to rain down on our heads. The British government froze all assets so that Rodney's father would have had to get permission to send his allowance. He did not get it. Rodney kept going to the Canadian consulate to find out if his reserve rank in England was valid in Canada. He had earned it at his school. The days passed, as static as a still shot of someone with a frozen leg forward. What we had in common, way beyond any current event (as they called it in my eighth-grade class), was an earned and long-lived terror of our parents. I had learned in a hard school to act first and tell afterward. So I kept on cleaning the apartment, waiting to get up the nerve to call my parents.

Within days of our descent into lower Manhattan, the telephone rang. It was my mother. She was so furious that she was whispering. She told me that I had broken my father's heart, that I was to come home at once, that there would be no more permission to cash emergency checks. How she found my tele-

---

[1] Since Rodney was a British citizen, he had to go to Canada to enlist in the British forces.—AHF.

phone number I will never know, but how they found out about Rodney and me was simply by opening the local Sunday paper.

One of the people I had hardly noticed crowded around the marriage-license window had been a freelance reporter who picked up tidbits for local papers. He had sent the news to Charleston. My parents threatened to sue the paper.

It must have been awful for them. I see them, sitting in bed on a Sunday morning, drinking the coffee that my father always made. It was his only domestic act in the week. Later she would go to church, and he would not. But he did say his prayers every night, on his knees beside their bed, with his elbows propped on his side of the bed and his hands flat together with his head resting on them, always, as if he were very tired. All their hopes for their daughter, hopes that I had never fitted, crashed down on their heads. The lovely wedding was gone, the nice house, the nice family, all that preparation, when I shied to the bit like a recalcitrant horse—the clothes, the dancing lessons, the touch of perfume in my pretty hair, the club around the swimming pool in the summer, Sweet Briar in the winter, gone. I had married a foreigner instead of a nice local boy.

Week after week trudged past before we could get to Canada. I went back to modeling. We had little married-couple dinners in the impersonal apartment. One of my dearest friends saw where we were living and lent us her apartment in the East Seventies when she and her husband went south, with all her beautiful plates and knives and forks and spoons, and all the presents from a large wedding for us to use, pretending. It was the best gesture in a lost time. Later, in another apartment in the same building, on the floor either below it or above it, I would watch the East River from George Plimpton's apartment during many of his parties.

But in that fall of 1939, Rodney and I waited in that building, suspended in time, until finally J. Walter Thompson allowed him to transfer to its Toronto office.

4

TORONTO

❧

The first thing I learned in Toronto in January was how to fall on the ice and not hurt the baby. I was wonderfully and happily pregnant, illogical as that may seem under the circumstances.

For months, Rodney had tried to join the Canadian army. As far as we were concerned, the war had stopped in its tracks. It had become dulled in our minds and everyone else's. Later, that period after the declaration of war and the invasion of Norway would be known as the "Phony War." For us it was someplace else, and we were faced with survival, as most of the world is day after day. We had tried to find the war and were stranded in some limbo of neither war nor peace. We were totally unprepared for this attrition and, frankly, this poverty.

Finally Rodney was offered a commission. It was then that I came up against a hierarchy within the brain of the Englishman that was an interior definition of himself. It was beyond personal, beyond genetic. I thought I had known about "we" and "they," which in the South depended on money, church, kinship. It was a children's game compared to the English self-image.

Rodney's father had raised him on an infinite pride of place as an officer in a "good" regiment. The memory of his mother, who had died when he was very young, was defined not as a person who had lived and died but as the niece of an earl. That, according to Rodney, who would have been horrified if I had called him a snob, was a definition of who he was.

He was furious at the offer, and his fury took the form of depression. It soon became both obvious and unavoidable that since Rodney was wrestling with refusal to accept the offer, it was time that I got up out of a well-remembered stuffed chair in the boardinghouse where we were living, pleased with myself and my dressing gown, and set out to find work.

When Rodney saw that I was looking in the *Toronto Globe and Mail* for some kind of job I could do, he went to the army and accepted the rank of lieutenant in the Army Service Corps, which was his other phrase for shame. Officer material didn't go into the Army Service Corps. Officer material joined a regiment. Our one room became a platform for the unfairness of the Canadian army, which was, after all, made up of provincials. It was so unlike Rodney that it seemed as if he had been taken over by another personality.

That personality was his father. He wrote to his father that he had joined up as a lieutenant, but he was afraid to tell him it was in the Army Service Corps. He went off in a creaking new uniform to the army camp at Lake Simcoe, north of Toronto, and I set out on my own to find a furnished apartment and a job.

Miss Addie, my grandmother, thought that the Catholic Church was the Whore of Babylon in the Book of Revelations. Nevertheless, she gave me advice that I took. She said that if you were in a strange place, you should go to the Catholic hospital, since they were always the best. So I went to the Catholic hospital and they sent me to a doctor who would "oversee" my pregnancy; they also told me that I would have to pay in advance for a place in the hospital when "the time came." That was explained sadly as something they had been forced to do by so many strangers coming to Toronto.

I saw an announcement in the *Globe and Mail* that there would be auditions at the Canadian Broadcasting Company. English actors were needed for a murder mystery. The radio play was called *The Mark of the Duke*.

I sat waiting my turn with a room full of actors or fakes like me who had emigrated to Canada. I can mimic voices. So I listened to the others speaking "English English," and when I went in for my audition, need overcame honesty, and my voice was as plummy as the best of them. I got the job of ingenue, which consisted mostly of screaming.

So every week when I got my paycheck, I took part of it to the hospital and lived on the rest in an apartment that belonged to a scholarly couple who taught at the university and were very fidgety about their belongings, none of which I remember, except that they were various shades of brown. I remember so little about it—a door, a narrow corridor, an "un-place."

But the way I commuted during the long months of pregnancy is with me still—not the number of the bus but the long ride past houses that seemed to be all the same size. I see myself standing, holding onto a strap on a bus from the grocery, the doctor, the CBC, growing bigger and bigger, and sometimes nearly in tears because none of the men would get up and let me sit down when it was obvious, to me at least, that I was eighteen months pregnant, alone in a strange country where the men had no manners, and missing the South where people had manners.

One day, a man sitting beside where I was straphanging

tugged at the tent I was wearing and said, "Wait here. I'm getting off at the next stop."

The next stop was about half a mile away. I was so furious, so weak, so pathetic, and so far from home that when he finally got up, I knocked him flat.

As for the director of *The Mark of the Duke*, he was tearing out what hair he had left because his ingenue was getting bigger and bigger. I finished the job two weeks before my son was born, sitting at a table leaning into the microphone because I was too big to get close enough standing. In the last episode, I was supposed to scream twice. They said I screamed three times. I didn't.

In the meantime, I was getting other jobs in radio, both commercial and CBC. The CBC one was called "Carry On, Canada." The lead speaker, who gave the cues, was an anchorman called Loren Green, who later became Lorne Green and was the daddy in the famous Western television show *Bonanza*.

Loren Green stood at the microphone surrounded by waiting actors. He would watch the light change from red to green—which, by the way, was one of the most nerve-wracking seconds in radio. Silence meant loss of money. I think it was called "dead air." Loren Green's hand was cupped to his ear so he could judge the timbre of his voice on the air. At the light change, he would begin the program in a beautiful, sonorous voice, calling out with verve and passion to remind Canada it was at war, "Carry on, Canada."

We all waited around him for our cues. I remember only one of my speeches, but it was like many of the others, which I was told to speak with verve and passion. So when he pointed his finger at me, I called out, "Five thousand ditty bags from the women of SASKATOON, SASKATCHEWAN!!" I was finally a professional actress.

There were other jobs, and there was trudging from one small advertising agency to another. The only moment I remember, outside of watching that ominous clock turn green, was a terrifying line that had to be said quickly and efficiently. It was, "The patient has been anesthetized with a novocaine adrenaline injection." Try saying *that* quickly and efficiently.

I earned enough to pay the rent and the hospital, and to eat. There was another glitch. We were in the hands of impersonal bureaucracy. For some lack of reason that nobody could find, Rodney was not paid for nearly six months. War had diminished into worry and survival. The landscape of our minds diminished with it into destructive fallow days.

But for me, I realize now, the other life that I would live until today as I write this was beginning to form as a tiny echo in my mind. I read a lot. And I began, without even thinking, to carry pen and paper with me—on the bus, in the street, waiting for my cues in radio jobs. Earning a living as an actress had become a daytime job without my being aware of it. The other me, the one who was alone and would be always, was growing as my son was growing within me. What I was becoming was only a glimmer that went on and off, sometimes for weeks, but when it was there, anxiety shriveled and left me in peace.

I began to write poetry. One of the questions most often asked of me is, "When did you know you wanted to be a writer?"

My answer has always been, "I never did." You don't "want" to be a writer. You are conscripted. *Wanting* to be a writer can mean only the so-called literary life, the recognition. For me, writing is the same time every morning, the room alone, the white paper, the timeless pitch of concentration. When I finish as much as I can do, I am sick with exhaustion, and I spend much of the rest of the day preparing to go the next morning to the place in my mind where I work, as one goes home. It is not enough to lie down and rest. Physical work is my saving grace when I finish the day's writing. In many a garden in several countries, I have planted, watered, and weeded on that fatigue. My son has had to share me with this time as he would have shared it with a brother or sister.

When Rodney came home on leave for the weekend and found the poetry I had written, he was furious. He threw it in the fire and said, "I am the writer here, not you." I guess it was the beginning of the coolness that came between us, although I did not recognize it at the time.

I remember only a few lines, and I know all of it had to do with war. Those lines are, for me, a recognition that it was not the second world war but the first that had found me.

At the green grown center of my memory lies Cambrai,
Carved there by only a story. I was not born, nor you,
But the earth fell under the fall of our fathers. . . .

Early Sunday morning, June 30, I began to have the labor pains I had been anticipating. Rodney was on a weekend pass. My bill at the hospital was paid. The doctor had been paid. I, a stranger like so many others the war had brought to the city, could get on with having a baby.

It was, to me, a never-to-be-forgotten miracle. I relive it. I remember no pain, although there must have been some. I only remember lying under a light, the doctor out of sight, and the clock high on the wall behind my head. I tried to push away an anesthetic a nurse was putting over my face—not because of the anesthetic but because I wanted to keep on looking at the clock. It was just before twelve.

When I awoke, I thought I had died. There was a crucifix

above me where the clock had been. God or one of the angels sat comfortably in a chair by the bed, all dressed in white.

It was Sister Benedicta, who told me later that she was the best poker player in the hospital. She also told me that I was the only Protestant in the delivery ward. But it wasn't a ward. It was a room, and a strange baby was in my arms. I was terrified that I would break him.

I was kept in the hospital for nearly two weeks; I remember this because Sister Benedicta, who had become a friend, told me that I was the only Protestant in the entire hospital on Orange Day.[1] Since I had no idea what Orange Day was, she was more than delighted to tell me about the Battle of the Boyne when King William of Orange defeated the Catholics at the Boyne River. It was the essential split between the north and the south of Ireland that has been going on ever since with as much verve as on the day of the battle. Hence the parade below my window when the Prots in their orange sashes marched past the Catholic hospital. Their marching band could have awakened the dead of the original battle.

A retired children's nurse was doing her Christian duty by accompanying young new parents home for the first two weeks. So I was chosen as the young new parent of the month, and she went home with me. The tiny new person who was so frightening had a name. He was a real person called Christopher (as his own name not connected to anybody in either fam-

---

[1] Orange Day is the day that Irish Protestants celebrate the victory of the forces of William III (or "William of Orange"), the Protestant king of England, Scotland, and Ireland, over the Catholics who were supporting his deposed father-in-law, James II of England (James VII of Scotland), in the Battle of the Boyne. By the calendar of the time, that battle—on the east coast of Ireland just outside the town of Drogheda—took place on July 1, 1690, but since the adoption of the Gregorian calendar in 1752 (which necessitated the addition of eleven days), it has been celebrated on July 12.—AHF.

ily), Henry for Rodney's father, Edward for my father, and
Weathersbee at the end.

The nurse, who was Irish, scared the milk out of me. She
was what today would be called a controller. She was used to
being obeyed. Her main order was, "Don't! It's bad for your
milk!" She made me drink Guinness stout so that the baby
would sleep through the night. Needless to say, her orders, plus
the worry that I didn't know how I was going to pay the rent,
dried me up, and Christopher went happily on to a big full bottle. Ten days after I got home from the hospital, three weeks
after his birth, I was modeling retail dresses in an expensive
women's dress shop on Bloor Street. I realized that the touch-
and-go of radio was too uncertain, and the modeling paid
every week.

At Christmastime, I worked in Eaton's Department Store,
the largest and grandest in Toronto. I was in the china department. The Canadians and their English cousins buy thousands
of bone-china teacups and saucers as Christmas presents. I
dreamed bone-china cups and saucers, Wedgwood. If you sold
a whole set, you got a bonus. I watched the others sell. They
stood on fine china plates to show how strong the seemingly
frail china was. I tried it and put my foot straight through the
plate, which was very expensive. I didn't know the trick of
standing only on the thick rim under the plate. I had to pay the
wholesale price, which left me with little of my fourteen dollars
a week.

One day an old, gnarled man came in to buy a teacup, or to
talk, mostly to talk. He was an itinerant gold prospector. He
even, he told me, had a claim in the Yukon. I was fascinated.
Here was a real Canadian. After he left, the manager told me
never to waste time talking to customers. On Christmas Eve,
the store stayed open until eight o'clock for those who had for-

gotten to buy the single teacups that would be collected to sit in cupboards unused but admired until their owners died. When I got on the bus to go home, I was so tired that I went to sleep and only woke up when the bus reached its final destination, about a mile from where I lived. It was the last bus. So I trudged through the cold and snow-slick streets of a Toronto that seemed deserted. When I got home, I was half frozen. Rodney opened the door to the apartment. He had come on leave as a surprise. He had trimmed a tree and put presents under it. It was a blessed thing for him to do.

I just stood in the middle of the room and began to cry. He didn't understand the tears of joy and relief. He thought I was criticizing him. I see these scenes in so many apartments in the city, played by those who married in the flood of war without knowing each other's needs or cares.

Toronto, the place many joked was fourteen suburbs in search of a city, had, suddenly and astonishingly, become an international city. The war was in the streets, the restaurants, and above all in the Royal York Hotel, which became known—almost in a day, it seemed—as the Royal Cork. No wonder the word *fall* was in my private mind, embedded there by the news of the fall of Belgium, the Netherlands, Norway. We had followed the retreat from Dunkirk when thousands of English boats, riverboats, ferries, leisure boats, fishing fleets—so many not meant for any water but local rivers and canals—went on their own across that dangerous water of the English Channel to pick up British and French soldiers under the attacks of the Stuka dive-bombers. Overhead, the newly trained children of the Royal Air Force fought their first air battles with the *Wehrmacht* pilots, so many of whom had had years of training assisting the forces of Franco in Spain. The wild channel played its part by suddenly, they say, becoming "as still as a mill pond." It was, and has not been discredited since in any way, the miracle of the survival of the British, Australian, and Canadian armies that turned the fall of France into a tragic victory. Instead of the 45,000 men expected to be rescued, 338,000 were taken back to England.

I made friends with a family who had escaped from France in that long, slow line of refugees we saw on the newsreels. Their daughter, who still spoke in whispers, from shock, told me about it, and told me again. One day she said, "A Frenchman will give his life for his country, but he won't give five francs for it." It told me more about the fall of France than any official news.

Toronto was so full of uniforms of various nations, including the British Royal Air Force cadets who were at flying schools around Toronto, that a German officer in uniform walked out the main gate of a prisoner-of-war camp, was saluted by the sentry, took a bus to Toronto, walked down to the Lake Ontario waterfront, hired a rowboat, and was about a mile on his way to the neutral American shore, twenty miles away, when he was caught.

I remember them all—passing in the street, cluttering the lobby of the Royal Cork, at quickly arranged parties in the rooms. I don't know how I was introduced to anyone, but I was, and I was lonely, and there were people who had really been to war. The blitz had begun over London, and the voice of Winston Churchill, the new prime minister, began to be imitated at parties in Canada. The voice was new, the sentiments as old as Shakespeare's Henry V: "We will fight in the streets. We will fight on the beaches. We will never surrender."

He spoke to me, and I know that almost everybody who heard him knew that he was speaking to them. That was Churchill's genius, that rolling Spenserian prose, so familiar to the English-speaking ear. With all the action someplace else, with all the horribly exciting bad news, we were in war, surrounded by it, engulfed in it.

One night I was standing, alone for one of those seconds when in a crowd everyone seems to retreat and leave one isolated. Someone was giving a party in a suite at the Royal Cork, crowded with student pilots, mostly English, on leave. Some spoke Spanish. It could have been a party given by the whole of the Argentine polo team, one of the world's best, with several ten goal players. They had come to Canada as a group to join the air force. They gave lots of parties.

The room was packed with caps with white flashes on them, the sign of student pilots; later I would think in RAF language and call them "sprogs." Somehow, one of the students and I fell into a conversation that seemed like a meeting of old friends. This was to happen often during that strange time. We spoke almost intimately, a private exchange of names, likes, and dislikes that was so underneath the noise that we seemed for a little while to be alone.

He was eighteen. I was an older woman, twenty-two. He said, "We are going to need everybody. My father says nothing will be the same," and then, changing the subject, "I am going to fly Spitfires. But there are new planes that can break the sound barrier. They aren't out yet. My father has seen them." It was not until the first jets were made public and Sir Frank Whittle's name became familiar that I remembered hearing about them first at a party full of familiar strangers in a suite at the Royal Cork Hotel in Toronto, Canada.

When the prototype engine was put on display at the Air and Space Museum in London, I examined it. A bobby pin was holding two of the connections together.

The student pilot's mind seemed to flip from one secret to

another, always beginning with, "My father . . . ," as if he were
edging toward something he had not yet said.

"If I am shot down, will you take my place?" he said suddenly. "I know I must find someone to do it. We all must." We
had known each other for an hour at most. "You see, women
are doing the ground jobs in the RAF. It frees the men to fly.
Will you?" he asked again.

"Yes," I told him, and we began to talk about horses, a safe
topic about which he knew a great deal. He told me about it as
if he wanted to store it in another mind for safety. We saw each
other a few times after that. It was as if I were conscripted as a
favorite aunt with whom he could practice the kind of adolescent flirting he would have done with older relatives in some
vast country house that he referred to but never bragged about.
It was the first time I had ever met an English aristocrat; later I
found that he had been true to form. It is a quality rare in the
United States—a directness, a simplicity, once they allow anyone within the high walls of their unself-conscious class. That,
and his habit of referring to a father far away who had warned
him that things would never be the same again, was our friendship. I could only compare it, looking back, with the straight
sense of equality that I had known in the country in West Virginia, mountain hospitality, mountain independence. But,
after all, he was an eighteen-year-old boy, and these things were
a strength and not a protection for him. He had just left Eton.

I needed to be at ease with somebody. Outside of weekend
leaves, Rodney and I were learning to live entirely apart; intimacy was destroyed by this fact and by our learning to be at
home in different worlds. As for what we did together, it was an
entirely celibate isolation. He still complained of the Army Service Corps. I began, I see now, to insult him by being patient
with his repetitions of complaints.

From the student pilot I received, as if it were a gift from a stranger, the open friendship that we both needed, an awareness of each other that could have, under other circumstances, been falling in love. It was, for both of us, the kind of adolescent affection I remember from school and the summertimes around the country-club pool. I remember, too, that we went to the movies to see *Sailors Three* and were hysterical with laughter. I dwell on this because it was so important to what became, later, a road to war for me.

In the winter, when Christopher was so small, it was bitter cold. I could not put him out in his carriage for more than a few minutes to get fresh air. For that reason, in the spring we moved into a small house near the Cricket Club where he could, as soon as he was able to stand, stay outside in a playpen and make speeches to passersby, of whom there were so few.

I made other friends, the best and longest with Helen Ignatieff, the one person I regretted leaving after Rodney was sent overseas to England. I would miss her, as you miss people you have known all your life.

These intimacies that mirrored the known of our pasts seemed to be needed by all of us who were displaced by the war, victims of indifferent choices by people we did not know existed, in the wrong place at the wrong time.

Christopher was sixteen months old when I went back to West Virginia to live with my parents. When I went to have him added to the American passport I carried—along with a British one, since I was considered a dual national—I was told that since he was born in Canada of an English father, he was not an American. But I had already learned to face and cope with the faceless rules. I simply asked for the book of laws that applied to American citizens, sat in the office—it must have been a consulate—and read through the vast set of rules that were positive, negative, crisscrossed each other, like a pyramid of negatives.

It took several hours, during which I refused to leave before I found what would help. I can still see where the obscure rule is on the page; it would be one of my aids to memory. A child born abroad of an American mother could reenter the country before the age of two as an American citizen. So Christopher had three nationalities by law—American, British, and Canadian. It would be a protection for him later.

5
PREWAR IN THE UNITED STATES, 1941-1942

∽

I would go through disenchantment twice on my return from
war to people who had not lived in its wake and who
resented a threatened upset to their lives. The familiar was a
shock. Relatives and friends whom I had known all my life were
now strangers. Roosevelt had instituted the first "peacetime"
draft in American history. Every night at the dinner table,
which was a forum and always had been, my parents argued.
For years, my brother Joe and I had listened and, like two
creeks, had been formed by the river of opinions. I had reacted
against almost everything my father said. He thought Franklin
D. Roosevelt—he always said the whole name in an argument
that had gone on since 1932—had led the country down the
path to hell. He simply stated it as a tragedy. I never heard him
raise his voice. It was not his way.

There were jokes about Britain. "Britain can take it," the
motto for the Battle of Britain, was changed at the parties to
"Can they dish it out?"

General Erwin Rommel's Panzer divisions were roaring
across North Africa, and it seemed to me that every mile they

took from the British army was pointed out. The "Desert Fox" was a negative hero.

I hated it, hated being there, more out of place than I had ever been before. Nobody seemed to know what it meant to go to war, and how could they? The atmosphere of the United States then was self-protective. Men like my father who had never been to war had opinions, and those who had survived World War I were silent. My parents had told the story so many times of the nurse coming into the hospital room a few days after I was born and saying that they had me to keep my father out of the draft. She called him a slacker. Slacker lists were published in the local paper. Could my intense, almost lemming-like insistence on joining up have been affected by it?

I felt censored in my family's brutally innocent company. It has taken me years to forgive them for the shock of being forced backward. My mother resented me, the war, the circumstances in which I had come home—in that order. She had thought herself rid of me, and there I was again, everything she disliked at the time when she wanted to enjoy her new house, her new peace, her new place with my father when she had to share none of his attention. I was frantic about its effect on Christopher. She, to whom all affection had always been a battlefield, vied for Christopher's attention, and the person she challenged for it was, of course, me.

The atmosphere was colder than the Toronto weather. I had no money to go anywhere else and take him. I was intent on doing something, anything, to help people so far away that to them they did not even exist, not daily, not in the night.

The nights were long until I was able, I thought, to find a solution that would create a better atmosphere for Christopher. My father adored him. My mother was affectionate with him when I was not there. Imogene, the maid who came every day but Sunday, was pleased, but I was told several times that she still thought I ought to marry somebody closer to home.

Imogene had been with the family since they had moved into the new house on the hill. She not only cleaned and ironed but also was the person who was chosen as the mouthpiece for some of my mother's opinions. My mother would make a little laugh, which warned without her knowing it that she was going to make up a story, and then she would begin, "Imogene says . . ." She said she had found Imogene crying in the garden when the news came about my marriage, and Imogene had told her, "I thought Miss Mary Lee would marry one of those nice Spilman boys across the hill. . . ." My mother never gave up on this idea. She was nothing if not possessed with patient anger.

If I am hard on my mother, I don't know how otherwise to tell what happened. I see now that she had every right to hope for the peace of her middle age without a daughter, a son, and a war intervening. She was a very honest woman, and it would have been beneath her image of herself not to let us all know how she felt.

At first I tried the only outlet presented to me for some kind of war work. It was called Bundles for Britain. It was an Anglophile joke, a country-club charity that consisted of selling little lapel pins like the RAF flashes sewn on the uniforms of air crews. The Battle of Britain had made them popular. There were even teacups, those damnable teacups, with pictures of the king and queen. Bundles for Britain drew the Anglophile snobs like flies to the honey of "war work."

I tried to join up in the British forces, even the merchant marine, to use the signals training that I had had in Toronto. I knew that there was no hope of joining the U.S. Army Air Force, as it was called then. I could not have passed the physical. I was, and have been since I was three years old, nearly blind in my left eye. It was straightened by an operation. My brother had always told me that my father had been repulsed by having a cross-eyed daughter.

Since I was an American citizen on American soil, I was not allowed to join a "foreign force." At night I fell into dreams, and at four o'clock in the morning, the time that Fitzgerald called hell, I even pondered the story of Solomon and the two women who fought over the child.

There were two moments that come back to me so clearly that I relive them, as when you remember little details of where you were when a disaster happened. In both of them, I was in the car with my father. In the first, we were crossing the bridge that haunts me to this day, and suddenly, as if I were watching the plane spiral out of the sky, I saw my so-young RAF friend shot down.

In the other, it was not a vision. My father and I were driving up the hill road toward their house, half listening to the Sunday Symphony on the car radio, when the broadcast was interrupted by the solemn voice of H. V. Kaltenborn, the never-to-be-forgotten: "This is H. V. Kaltenborn. . . . The Japanese Air Force has attacked Pearl Harbor. . . ."

My brother is standing with his hands on the back of a chair near the fireplace in the new Queen Anne house. He is as straight as if he were on parade rest at Virginia Military Institute, where he had gone to college. This is not his usual stance. He usually lounged well, even when he was standing or walking. He announces solemnly that he is going to enlist. My father shakes hands with him as if he doesn't know him very well. I am having hysterical giggles on the sofa. My mother has turned to ice.

I went to Washington, to the British Embassy. I walked up to a desk—I've forgotten which one—and asked if I could see someone to enlist. The young man telephoned, as if he were totally unsurprised at strangers turning up at the embassy to volunteer. I gathered later that I had been one of the very few who had made that mistake, which had been the high point of a boring day for them.

The assistant army attaché came out and shook my hand. Then I was in an office with the assistant army attaché, the assistant air attaché, and the assistant naval attaché, two of whom were on rest assignments after their tours of duty. One of them was Roald Dahl, a Hurricane fighter pilot who had been shot down in the African desert. He later began a successful career by writing about the gremlins, those tiny figures in the air glimpsed, they swore, by pilots in the RAF. The only problem he ran into as a diplomat was his language. He had been sent to Washington speaking RAF, which was, at times, sewer, and sometimes *haute* sewer. Later, when I got out of the WAAF, I used the same language. In moments of stress, I still do.

Also in the room where I was being interrogated was Squadron Leader Ben Travers, England's most famous writer of bedroom farces, who was to become one of my dearest friends all through the war. Of all the people I met then in Washington, he was the one I loved most. He had been an ace in World War I. He taught me how to behave, and to sing World War I songs. His moral advice was, and he made me promise to keep it, "Sleep with who you want, for love or fun or drink or politeness. But promise me you will never sleep with anyone out of boredom. That," he said, "is immoral."

On that first day, they considered me quite seriously. They decided that while I would "have more in common" with the WRENS, the Women's Royal Navy, their white stockings would hide my legs, which would be a shame. The army was completely out of the question, "conscripts from the East End, don't you know." It has been forgotten that every woman in England on her eighteenth birthday was conscripted for the WAAF, the WRENS, the army, or the land army. So my volunteering for the WAAF, the Women's Auxiliary Air Force, was an English trifle of snobbery, style, and class.

Since I had to have a job while I waited to be sent overseas, I was sent to the British Purchasing Commission, where I was plunged without training, as so many thousands were, into a taut and urgent connection with the fighting war. Washington had been crowded ever since Lend-Lease.[1] There were thousands of soldiers, as there had been in Toronto, in offices, sharing taxis, on passes or on leave from Camp Lejeune or Quantico.

Many of those in the British forces were from the Africa campaign, which was going so badly. When I first got there, there was still discussion about Churchill's replacing Claude Auchinleck with a little weasel of a man named Montgomery.

Not only the streets, but the offices were overcrowded. Washington had been thrust into war before war had begun. The British Purchasing Commission was in two offices in an unofficial business building. I remember room for three desks in the larger one. Nothing was there to impress, only men working so hard and so short-staffed that when my new friends at the embassy called, I was sent down at once, unprepared— which would be a pattern I saw all through the war—to file the papers for the rush to send equipment to Cairo for the British army's planned attack on Rommel.

[1] President Franklin D. Roosevelt signed the Lend-Lease Act on March 11, 1941. Through this program, the United States would supply Britain, the Soviet Union, China, and other Allied nations with war materiel until V-J Day, on September 2, 1945.—AHF.

There were lots of pictures of General Montgomery, whose egocentric vision of himself was as a common soldier, too busy to make a grand fuss like some others with their limousines and their flags. All this was pointed out until Montgomery became the man he had planned to be. I learned what the word *scramble* meant in wartimese.

So, by the most tenuous of connections, I filed the papers that registered the orders to start the flow of arms for the victory that would be El Alamein.

We all went to long lunches and embassy parties and, from time to time, worked through the night. At first I lived with the head of the commission and his wife, both very attractive and very social. It was also the cold bath of recognition that I was still a minority of the few in the war, that most were there because it was war, not because it was a right side or a wrong side, as we all had thought during the Spanish war.

Toward the end of that frantic, elegant time, I lived with four WAAF officers in a tiny house in Georgetown, any one of hundreds that look so alike I can no longer find it. They had all been at Biggin Hill, the central airfield during the Battle of Britain. Two of them were widows of pilots. Three of them had left their children with their own parents, and they assured me that this was happening all over England, so young women could serve. It assuaged, but only a little, my guilt about leaving Christopher. I had not meant to live so grandly, but it was easy to fall into wartime instant grandness in Washington. For me, at twenty-three, it consisted mostly of riding taxis on expenses—since we were always supposed to be in a hurry—dressing up a lot, which I have always liked, and getting used to talking to well-known people at cocktail parties.

Ambassador and Mrs. Maxim Litvinov were very popular. They came to many of the parties and seemed very pleased to be there. The Soviets were all party-loving people except for the two UGPU agents who followed the ambassador and his wife wherever they went. They were known in Washington as "Twee-dle Dum" and "Tweedle Dee." Ambassador and Mrs. Litvinov had a habit of making their ambassadorial rounds for ten min-utes and then seriously moving to the hors d'oeuvres table and eating their dinner.

I was learning almost too fast for any ease that all those who were so comfortably intent on fighting the war were not what I had expected. Many of them would have agreed with the less obsessional of the *Wehrmacht*. I had an office mate named Phoebe who set out to mind my manners. She was the most British person I had ever met. She was from Buenos Aires. When she found out I knew the Argentine polo team, she was suddenly warmer to me than she had been. One day, she heard me making a date for lunch. When I hung up, she turned to me, horrified: "Mary Lee! You are not going to lunch in public with a niggah!" I said, and I will not use his real name, "Phoebe, [Blank Blank] is a Hindu Brahmin, and if he goes to lunch with me or you, he has to take a three-month religious cleansing cure when he returns to India for having lunch with an untouchable. He says his grandmother insists."

So the trivial mixed with the frightening and the urgent while I waited, and because I was waiting to go to England, I was treated as if I were the only young woman doing so curious a thing. The fact that there were millions of eighteen-year-old girls conscripted in England had not surprised them. Those who were wartime additions to a prewar diplomatic world had to learn quickly. As a result, the turnover at the British Embassy was quite quick.

One of the aides was answering the telephone in Detroit when the British ambassador, Lord Halifax, had gone there to try to persuade the automobile union leaders to help with the newly formed Lend-Lease program. When some of the union leaders turned up at the hotel asking to see Lord Halifax, the aide told them, "His lordship cannot see you. He is hunting today." Detroit was entertaining him with a stag hunt. The aide-de-camp was abruptly sent back to England, which pleased him. He was to be a friend who rescued me when, finally, I got there.

The lights were on all night at the Soviet Army headquarters. The invasion of the Soviet Union by Hitler was costing thousands of Russian lives. Sherman tanks to Russia, planes to England—there was a constant flow of American-produced goods to the Allies.

I was to become part of it.

6

THIRTEEN MONTHS IN THE WAAF

⌇

At last, early in October, my posting came through. The act of going aboard the *City of Benares* is so clear that I see the sky at twilight, the darkening deck of the small ship with its lascar crew and its louvered doors designed for the tropical waters of the passage to India in peacetime.

That first evening, I stood beside a merchant mariner, leaning on the rail and watching the lights of Manhattan from Pier 1, at the bottom of the island. I had a Mae West, the issued life jacket, over my arm. He looked at it.

He said, "Throw that away. The water in the North Atlantic will kill you from cold in ten minutes."

He was one of a large group of survivors of German submarine attacks in the South Atlantic and the Caribbean. Some of them had been torpedoed several times. They were being sent back to England to take ship again. Some were so nervous that if anything was dropped near them that made a sharp noise, they jumped. Some of them screamed.

We crossed the North Atlantic in a slow, four-knot convoy. The ships spread across the endless ocean in a great square, the edges of it almost out of sight across the horizon. We were in the center of the convoy. There was a flight of Fleet Air Arm navigators aboard, as well as mothers and children going back to England. Some of them had found their exiles to safety in the Caribbean islands worse than being at home and subjected to the bombings. They, the Fleet Air Arm, the merchant marine survivors, and one other couple made up the ship's complement. The lone couple was, I think, going "home" from some kind of government duty in the islands. They took me aside, complained about the rest of the passengers, and invited me to join them as the only person they could see aboard who had anything "in common" with them. It was my first exposure to that hard-edged English class snobbery.

I chose the Fleet Air Arm. One of them, a Scotsman of about twenty, told me I was a fool to do what I was doing, that I had no idea what I was getting into. He said he had been in Germany at the beginning of the war for a year as part of a spy trio. He spoke no German, so the others concealed him behind a story of being struck dumb by the bombing of—I remember Antwerp as the place he named. The trio had had fifteen minutes to meet a plane at a hidden airfield in northern Italy as a rendezvous to get home. It sounded amateurish to me, a story from *The Boy's Own Paper*. But that is who fought on our side of World War II, the amateurs in their standard-issue uniforms. He had joined the Fleet Air Arm as soon as he returned.

For the rest, we sang songs and poured gin into the water coolers, since the bar was only open once a day.

In the mornings, we checked the "coffin corner" to see whether the ship in the most vulnerable position had been torpedoed during the night. Sometimes we heard it, a low, far-distant thunder. Sometimes we knew by the ships' changing places in the convoy. In between the lines of merchant ships taking supplies to England, sleek Canadian corvettes patrolled, slim-lined like barracuda.

We sailed north of Iceland and entered the Irish Sea from the north to land at Liverpool. The harbor at Liverpool was a graveyard of lost ships, their sites marked by the tip of a mast, a prow, or a stern jutting up from the dark water.

It was not until years later that I found that we had been part of a decoy to draw submarines away from the transport of the first American troops to cross the Atlantic. It was the beginning of the North African invasion.

I wrote about my service in the WAAF, the Women's Auxiliary Air Force of the RAF, in my book *All the Brave Promises*, which was published in 1966. In it I tried to tell not necessarily about my experience as a WAAF but rather about me as an observer of a whole contingent of young English women who had been drafted on their eighteenth birthdays.

I was self-urged into writing it then by the fact that the use and sacrifice of millions of English women was being forgotten in the official peacetime bravery, fake crises, and bragging of the Cold War, the self-congratulation of it, its terrible mistakes.

It was such a tiny arrow thrown, but it was all I could do.

Now, the memory of that experience has changed into almost total recall. It is happening to so many of us; memories become stronger the farther away they are, so deep within the body and spirit that it is all relived.

So, sixty years later, I will try to tell about some of the time and the place and myself there in a way I did not do before. Although I was trying then to be the seer for the reader, and although much of this experience was described in *All the Brave Promises*, there was not the final thing, the "what it did to me," how it sculpted me into beginning to become the person that I have grown toward being ever since then.

I have never written without the lit fuse when intention

turns into demand, and I know I cannot rest until I am committed to the vision and its questions. It has happened every time, and it is happening this time, when I am trying to trace the path that led me into being the writer I have become.

I want to tell something of what happened to me as part of the road I have taken through my life, which has produced the work I have done, for better or worse. For those who remember *All the Brave Promises*, some of what comes back to me now, either to haunt or to heal, will be repetitive.

I was given my last lunch at Prunier's by a friend who suggested that she pay for the food and I pay for the wine. This would not have stuck in my memory, or been told in the former book and repeated here, had I not, as a result, gone into the WAAF with a shilling and had to walk from St. James's Street to Kingsway Recruiting Station.

I felt, although I would not have admitted it at the time, as if this were the right and proper thing to do, the way to be. I was joining the majority. My father had worked away his health to provide me with what was considered to be privilege, and it had become, to me, a prison. It was the way I looked and walked and spoke, the healthy color of my body, the Anglo-Saxon Gothic way that opened doors and froze the enemy when used to advantage. I had been ashamed of the advantages I carried in my body.

So, dragging my suitcase for that mile or so, I lengthened my stride and felt pride in beginning the vast luxury of being unknown by anyone with whom I would serve. Along St. James's Street by Lobb's and rain-soaked, half-burst sandbags, down Piccadilly, through Piccadilly Circus, around Leicester Square I marched, all of it as new to me as a dream, finally down the Strand past the Savoy to Kingsway Recruiting Station.

I was at least a head taller than any of the frightened and loudly brave girls gathered there to receive their assignments as their eighteenth-birthday presents from the king. We were made to line up by a female sergeant who had done it so many times she didn't look at us.

An important male in uniform went along the raggle-taggle line offering the King's Shilling, the age-old traditional token for joining up. I took pride as an American in refusing it. Nobody noticed this fine gesture but me.

We queued up for yet another physical exam. I failed my eye examination. I was refused. Before I could quite realize what was happening, I was standing on the pavement outside the recruiting station with my suitcase. I had left my trunk with evening clothes and other necessities at one of the family homes of the friend with whom I had had lunch. It was at the richest end of Carlton House Terrace. I saw myself going there, all bedraggled, among those I would later learn to call "the nobs." Their butler was as formidable as Cerberus, and a shilling would not have done at all.

The Air Ministry was at the corner. There was nothing to do but go and see a very young air commodore I had known in Washington who had returned to a job there. So much for the casting off of the Anglo-Saxon cloak of privilege.

His first words were, "My God, old girl, you made it!"

I said, "Not quite."

Having exploded by telling me, "They can't do that! Don't the bleeders know you've come all this way?" He said, "Wait here."

I didn't answer that where I had just been for half an hour nobody gave a damn, which was both healthy on their part and a profound fact for me to face.

He was gone for no more than half an hour. I rested,

calmed down, and looked out of his window at Kingsway, which I had never seen before. I tried to tell myself I was IN LONDON, but I'm afraid I didn't listen. I was too intent upon the door.

It finally opened and a joyful air commodore came in with another officer, both higher in rank than I would see again for many months.

"We have the answer," one of them said. "Here. Do you mind signing this chit?"—or some such question. Anyway, I had heard the first word of RAF slang, *chit*, a little piece of official paper, anything from a weekend pass to a ticket of delivery to a consignment of fighter planes from Canada or the United States. Many a chit had I filed in Washington, and now I had my own.

It instructed the recruiting sergeant to let me into the WAAF, that if I were totally blinded in action, I would only claim a half-pension. Since the full pension was at that time about three pounds a week, I signed with some relief and disappeared into the Women's Auxiliary Air Force of the Royal Air Force, where I was known as Aircraft Woman 2nd Class 2146391.

At Paddington Station, whose glass roof had been blown to pieces, I waited with the others, watched over by military police in case, I suppose, we ran away. On the train, I watched the strange country of England to the west of London slip by. I sat with a "flight" of several hundred eighteen-year-olds, in a carriage with seven new WAAF, still in their *civvies* (RAF slang), who all stared at me as if they were at the zoo and then began to chatter among themselves.

We slowed down to pass through Reading Station. I put my face against the window to try to see the jail through the early November mist. The girl across the aisle finally spoke to me: "Wa're ye lookin for?"

I answered truthfully, "The jail."

She answered proudly, "Me bruver's in there. Wat did your lot do?" She was settling down for a conversation that I couldn't have. How could I tell her that I was looking for the place where Oscar Wilde had served his sentence?

We went through initial training at RAF Hereford, a few miles outside of the small and beautiful city of Hereford. After initial training, I was sent, I mean *posted*, to RAF Hullavington, the Empire Central Flying School in Wiltshire, about seven miles from the town of Chippenham.

I lived, made friends, and worked as a ground-to-air signals operator for most of the thirteen months I served. It is, looking back, a kind of small miracle, how those of us who spoke a language, who knew the same books, the same music, floated toward each other out of the anonymity of a very large station.

An airman from Cambridge, who had been drafted out of the university into the first totally unprivileged life he had ever faced; a young newspaper reporter from Fleet Street, bright and edgy with opinions, who was a dear friend to me and told me off from time to time when I made a misstep, which was often.

One evening in the NAAFI,[1] the pub for the use of other ranks, where we could get food of a kind and beer of a kind, I made a comment about the WAAF sergeant who bawled out our numbers, never our names, in a piercing Cockney voice, when the orders for the sausage and mash, the fish and chips, the coffee, the never-ending jam rolls were ready. She had a mouth and a voice like a foghorn on the Thames on a misty

[1] NAAFI is the acronym for the Navy, Army, and Air Force Institute, created by the British government in 1921 to operate recreational facilities and sell goods to servicemen and -women and their families. Commissioned officers were not supposed to use it.—AHF.

day. I made the mistake of saying, in trying to be understanding of her, that she couldn't help her terrible voice. He laughed, "You really are a bloody awful snob. She's an individual, you dumb bastard. Her sister probably has a voice as dulcet as a bird."

There were many moments of learning like that. Never to ask for the salt by saying, to a table of airmen, "Are you all through with the salt?" *Through*, in English English, means a direction, not a finish. Small boys made tiny fortunes in London waiting until American soldiers on leave went into those red phone booths, put their money in the slot, and then walked out of the booth, cursing, when the operator said, "You're through." The small boys would rush in and push button B, catching the money as if they were playing a slot machine.

Then there was the Padre, the first Jesuit I ever knew. Before I had better sense than to try to argue with one on any subject that touched his training, I remember once saying, "I think I want to be a Christian Communist." He answered, "Oh, I am already one," which ended that foolishness. I was always so glad to see him, and he me; most people avoided the Padre. We were both lonely.

Then there was the ever-adoring medic assistant, a rangy boy not put together very well, who was the most radical Communist on the station. A friend as a joke had given me a record of the Red Army Choir, with rousing military folk music, and one night when I was playing it on the only phonograph on the station, in the so-called library, he heard it and rushed in. He had found a soul mate, and nothing I could say removed that delusion. When I left the station, I gave him the record.

There was the trade-union leader from Oxford, who worked at the Morris Automobile works. He was the first person I had ever met from Oxford, and it gave me a narky attitude toward the university I never quite lost. *Narky* means "anarchistic" in Cockney.

There were no right-wingers in the other ranks, except for a belligerent quintet of small girls from the East End whose parents were Mosleyites, and when they saw me, they tended to run toward me in a line, as if they were dancing the *palais glide*, stop dead in front of me, stare at somewhere around my navel to scare me, and then trudge off.

My job was to sit on watch in the Flying Control Room, with earphones connected to a Marconi transmitter-receiver, relaying orders from voices in the air to the flying control officer from pilots landing, taking off, sometimes lost, sometimes with wounded aboard. We kept every word from the air, every order from the Flying Control Room, in a logbook. My fellow WAAF on duty was a charming, friendly girl from Aberdeen with a soft Scottish accent, in which she told me that the people of Aberdeen spoke the most "pairfect" English in the British Isles.

Usually there were training exercises, called circuits and bumps, and sometimes there was night flying when the student pilots landed and took off from a dim **V** of ground lights that hardly pierced the vast blackout of the country around us. We sat enclosed with blackout curtains over the windows, so we saw nothing; our whole concentration was on the thin voice that came through the earphones, the language of height told in "Angels," the "Hello Nemo" call from lost planes, and the endless waiting, the essence of war. So much of RAF code has been taken into the language that it is hard to remember that it was once secret in order to protect lives.

Since we were on watch together, we also roomed together. Eight hours on, eight hours off, so that sleep was dictated by the flying control, not the day or the night. Sometimes, when I came off duty after the midnight-to-eight shift, I had some of the early day to myself, and I rode around the country roads on an issue bicycle to learn where I was. Sometimes, a pilot about to fly would call out, "Want to go for a flip?" And I would rush to the hangar where the parachutes were given out, put one on, and run, as it bounced against my bottom, to the plane—always a training plane, a Miles Magister with two open cockpits; a Miles Master, closed; or an Oxford, one of those twin-engine planes that are still used in the Caribbean and are known as grasshoppers, because so many of them are smuggling marijuana.

There were two kinds of pilots at the station—those very young, who were doing their last training flights in Oxfords before they were sent on active duty, and those a few years older but a generation older in memory, exhausted from the early days of the Battle of Britain, or service in Africa or that terrifying place then, Malta. They were a different breed. Sometimes one crashed and was buried in the churchyard at Stanton St. Quintin, where my watch mate and I were billeted. I could hear the slow march coming from the station, then the silence in the churchyard, the near-whisper of the Padre's voice. The coffin was sometimes far too small for a man, a boy, who had plunged from "Angels three" into the earth. When the coffin had been lowered into its grave, the quick march faded away as the guard returned to the station.

In the sky above England, the Miles Magisters were the last of the planes that flew slowly enough for the purest flying of all—watching the world below, turning, spinning so that the far ground was above us and below us or sliding fast beside us. There was the greatest sensation of speed nearest the ground. It slid by, then raced by, and then flew below us a green or red or yellow stream, not jet stream but field stream. From "Angels one," we watched as the ruins of Malmesbury Abbey, tiny below us, whirled, tossed among the fields that were squares or slips or long trails of yellow corn or green wheat or bright red poppies, and I thought then of World War I, for I was really seeing poppy fields below me, in planes that were much the size and speed of the old World War I "kites" of wood and cloth.

In these training planes we floated with the sky and the trailing clouds; we were not knifing through them. It is strange that, with the breaking of the sound barrier and the speed of the modern plane, we have lost touch with much of the sensation of speed itself, the hedgehopping, the manual sense of earth. Once, I think because the powers-that-were had to fight boredom and give the ground crews the sensation of being military, a route march was organized. Planes were to simulate dive-bombing and everybody was to lie flat on the ground as they passed over. I was in one of the planes; the pilot flew it so close to the ground that I could see the separate grass blades at the wingtip.

Later, when I went into the NAAFI, I heard airmen at the next table say, "That plane nearly crashed. There was a WAAF in it, too. . . ." How could we have crashed? For a few seconds we had owned the air, the earth, the grass, and all that was in it. Those times of flying taught me a little of that airfree security beyond bravery, that deceptive control of the sky, for a while, that the pilots knew and that sustained them.

I think it was out of deep weariness and boredom that several of the instructors, some of whom had been in the Battle of Britain or stationed in Africa or Malta, older than they should have been in their early to mid-twenties, decided that I should be trained for transport command. This was one of the most dangerous unsung jobs in the war. Women pilots ferried many of the planes to individual airports, and some flew across the

Atlantic from Canada or the United States. They flew unarmed in what could at any moment be hostile air.

It was a heady time for me, and it didn't last long. When the problem of a medical exam came up, as I had known it would, I tried to defuse it by saying I had signed on to have only a half-pension if I were blinded.

The pilot who was questioning me blew up. He informed me that he didn't give a damn, that I needed two eyes to land a plane. I countered weakly by saying, "Wiley Post only has one eye, and besides you told me to look at the horizon, not straight down."

It didn't work.

"Wiley Post pranged and killed himself and Will Rogers."

I failed. But before the medical, I had airborne instruction in the lovely open Miles Magister. I learned maneuvers in the air, approach, takeoff, with the instructor's hand as well as mine on the stick in his cockpit. It was during that time that I went hedgehopping in an Oxford and experienced the greatest sensation of speed known: the earth becomes water, fast flowing, an arm's touch just below.

One day I accepted a bet with an instructor. He told me there was a World War I maneuver that could only be done in a Magister. He called it an aerial *ozzle-twizzle*. He bet me I couldn't go through it without having a nosebleed. Since my nose had never before bled in a dive, I took the bet.

I was in the front cockpit of the plane. We were over an empty field, green, it must have been early wheat. We were at about "Angels one," a thousand feet. The instructor put the plane into a roll and the earth whirled around us—the field overhead, beside, underneath. He came out of the roll in a steep dive. We were totally still. The ground rushed toward us. Suddenly, at about a hundred feet, he threw the stick forward and we began to climb. I looked down at my uniform. I lost the bet. It was covered with blood.

This late in life, I need to try to understand what happened. It was not frightening. It was exciting, a heavenly surge of joy. A success. I know now that it was part of being there, unconnected with anything I had ever known, the earth, the air, the country, the people I lived with. It wasn't that it was all unreal. It was transcendently real.

There is a paragraph in *All the Brave Promises* that I want to quote here. It concerns a day in late summer when I was cycling along a back road in Wiltshire, in the sun, through the ripe fields, just ambling along thinking nothing:

> [For] the first time I sensed an irresponsibility, an ease of letting go. My uniform was issue, my bicycle was issue. I was utterly without worry about where my food was coming from. So long as I did what I was told, kept silence and remained acquiescent, I had freedom from decision, freedom from want, freedom from anxiety for survival. That, too, seemed out of my hands—the decision of an abstract, an order from "above." For a few minutes the rose hedges swept past me; I felt an almost mystic contentment. Then, even in the sun, cold fright caught me and I pedaled faster, as if I could ride away from the space of that feeling. I had experienced the final negative freedom, that of the *slave*.

Not many weeks later, an event made me see, without fear or hope, what blind, defective, personal authority could do. The commander of the group, of which Hullavington was one station, was himself coming up for being "bowler hatted," forced to retire, because of a whispered inefficiency in his command in Malta. A letter had come across his desk, marked by a censor. The commander had been responsible for the court martial of a young Canadian airman for "spreading dissent in a major dominion."

The airman had written to his family in Canada that WAAF were being punished by pack drill, by being marched "on the double" around the huge parade ground with full pack. This punishment was instituted by a new WAAF officer, who was soon afterward transferred when it was proved that she made the WAAF wash the coal in the bins.

The result of the airman's sentence and the WAAF pack drill had been an act of "dumb insolence"—King's Regulations words for a silent revolt. When the punishment happened, all airmen and -women stayed away from the parade ground, or turned their backs on the humiliating solo march of the small RAF prisoner, around and around the parade ground under the yells of a WAAF sergeant.

The airman was sent for a month to Chorley Detention Barracks, an RAF prison that was just about to break into a public scandal for its treatment of inmates. This brutal sentence became a cause in a community that needed a cause.

In *All the Brave Promises*, I referred to the Canadian airman as an unknown boy who would become an unknown man. After the book came out in 1966, I received a letter, one of the most valuable I have ever received.

It began, "I am the unknown boy who became an unknown man. . . ." He had become a lawyer in western Canada, and he wrote to thank me because he had never before thought, in that terrible impersonal time, that anyone had cared or noticed what was happening to him. I think there is a part of me that has been writing for him ever since.

At the time, I asked for a posting to another station. While

I waited, I was given *jankers* (punishment) by the same WAAF officer for being part of a group who cycled silently by every time the airman was marched past, flanked by four large sergeants. I was made to run along behind a tiny sergeant on her bicycle, on the way to scrub the living room of the officers' mess. There were broken records all over the floor. They had had a party.

I had only been at Bourton-on-the-Water—known as "Clamp Hill" for its dangerous mists, which hid the landing strip—for about a month when one evening, coming back on the air force bus from a day off, I suddenly cramped so violently and in such fierce pain that I couldn't move. I was carried off the bus into the sick bay.

I had been there a few days when the young doctor who looked after me and a ward full of other people came and perched on the end of the bed with his feet up.

He asked, "Have you been having dreams of being on watch?" I said I had. And then I explained that my roommate, on watch with me, talked in her sleep to phantom voices coming from planes.

"So do you, love," he told me. "You are suffering from signals shock from the enemy jamming."

Then he said, "You're bloody lucky. You can work your ticket. Do you know anybody in London?"

I said I did.

"Now I'm going to give you two weeks' sick leave. I want you to look for a job that will get you seconded to a cushy job in London. They won't put you back in signals. And you're not sick enough to be invalided out. All they will do with you is put you in admin, where you will give out patched shoes for the rest of the war." He sat for a minute more and then said sadly, "I wish I could work my fucking ticket. I'm fucking browned off."

I was exhausted, my nerves jangled from signals shock, and enmeshed in the discipline, the deprivation of the forces.

I was lucky that I knew people, unlike the others I was leaving behind. Ever since, I have felt twinges of guilt when I think about it. So, thanks to Herbert Agar, the Pulitzer Prize–winning editor of the *Louisville Courier-Journal*, and a friend in Parliament, a month later I was on my way to the train for London in the back of the RAF lorry with my "ticket"—my discharge "at own request"—in the pocket of the civilian clothes I had worn when I joined up.

The only thing left of my uniform was a pair of issue clodhoppers. Later I took great pleasure in wearing them once in a while so that female WAAF MPs would try to pick me up as a deserter, and I could show them my ticket.

There was another souvenir from my service in the WAAF, not so easily discarded. I shook when I heard a surprise noise, and once, when a radio technician in London turned to the frequency that was jammed, I fainted at the sound. I tended to scream when a door slammed, or someone knocked, or the dog scratched at the door when I didn't expect it. It is an entirely involuntary reaction to an unexpected noise. I still have it.

I left my station in the Cotswolds on a Saturday as Aircraft Woman 2nd Class 2146391 with a one-way ticket to London, three pounds, and a pair of issue shoes. On Monday morning, I reported for duty as a "simulated major" in the U.S. Office of War Information.

The OWI was in Carlos Place, conveniently across from the finest hotel in London, the Connaught, in one of the streets that lead into Grosvenor Square, known to the British then as Eisenhower Platz. The "simulated major" rank was protection—since we could be exposed to being captured—in case the Germans (I still called them "Jerries") raided Carlos Place to take us prisoner.

There was also a vast mountain of pay. All it meant to me was that I could get cigarettes by the carton at the Post Exchange (PX), so I no longer needed to smoke Woodbines with a pin when the butt was too short to hold.

Under American law, I had lost my citizenship when I joined a foreign army. And so, one morning, along with five members of the Eagle Squadron—Americans who had joined the RAF as pilots—I stood before the U.S. consul and forswore "allegiance to foreign potentates or princes." I was officially American again. All of us were classed as "premature anti-fascists," a description in which I still take pride.

7

LONDON, 1944

∽

O n Monday morning, I stood at attention beside a col-
league's desk and asked to be excused to go to the loo.

"Honey," he said, "you're out of the army. You can pee
whenever you want to."

What we both found in London then was controlled by
where we came from. Did we come on leave, away from the cold
and boredom and waiting of the military to the luxury of London, of baths and pink gin and some worn remains of graceful
living? Or had we newly arrived from America to the first
glimpse of the danger and deprivation of a city at war?

I had done both of these; in the late fall of 1943, the city I
came to was not my second London but my third.

When I arrived on leave, the first time, without enough
money to call my friends, since my whole week's salary was not
enough to tip the butler, I was free. I learned the streets. I wandered there in the anonymity of my air force blue uniform. It
was then that I had found the noontime concerts at the
National Gallery, the cheap food at the NAAFI, and what was
left of the London of Dickens, of Shakespeare, so familiar to
me that I hardly had to ask a direction, even though I had never
seen it before.

I had walked through miles of London streets, all during the day and into the blacked-out night. Osbert Sitwell wrote that the blackout made a medieval city of London. It didn't. There were no pine torches, no wax candles shining through windows to defeat the darkness. Instead, it was the opposite. London was plunged into the terrible present century and lay exposed under an open, dangerous sky.

The darkness was full of noises, the echoes of footsteps, of people talking, the cries for taxis. Sound itself seemed amplified and dependable in the blindness of the street. The smell was of dust, of damp plaster in the air, and of the formaldehyde scent of the dirty coal smoke that lodged in the yellow fog. The stained sandbags, the rust, the dull, peeling paint, damp that made great abstract blots down the walls, made London seem like a long-neglected, leaky attic.

The pitch darkness was inside rooms, as if they were caves deep under ground before the blackout curtains were drawn and the lamps were lit.

Outside, in the street, London became country again under a changing sky. The buildings were dark monoliths; the streets, steep canyons between cliffs. There were snaggled, bombed-out gaps in the townhouse rows that let in the moonlight through high windows that had once been such private rooms—here a fragment of wallpaper with faded, rain-streaked animals of a nursery, there a toilet, still precariously clinging to the wall, a towel left on a rack three stories high, drab in the rain.

Many of the ancient churches were only ruins that looked like stone lace etching the night sky. During the blitz, they had been low on the priorities of the firefighters. To new arrivals in London, it seemed pitch black outdoors, too, but not, by 1943, to Londoners.

People had become conscious again of the phases of the

moon, the light from stars. They had regained their "country eyes."

The third time I had come from a world where I had had to choose either to grow to love the lash or live in a secret anarchic world in order to survive. I had chosen the latter. After all, the almighty King's Regulations covered everything from hanging to corset covers (brassieres) for the use of WAAF. There seemed to be no way that a mere human could obey all the rules. It took time to learn to trust these new people.

The new London I found that first week was as heady as champagne: comfort, good food, clean American people after the months of loneliness, and a glamour that I had not expected. Almost everybody was old at the Office of War Information, or so they seemed at first. They were professionals; some were famous. They had come from *The New York Times*, the *Paris Herald Tribune*, from prewar publishing when it was an art, from the *Louisville Courier-Journal*, *Harper's Bazaar*, to name only the ones I remember. There they were, those who had wangled their way into war, at the wrong place, doing—in excesses of patriotism or curiosity or self-proof—work that was the wrong work at the wrong time. They had chosen to be in London through the attrition of the days, the "little blitz," the buzz bombs, the V-2s, and the debilitating atmosphere of neglect, dirt, and exhaustion that had built up over nearly four years of war.

They were valuable in some terms I had not run into as an aircraft woman. I, who had been hired as a "writer," had no experience at all beyond a few poems, a few short stories, all unpublished, all long since lost. I was, to them, an oddity, a rescued fragment. I was as fake as my simulated rank. One of my bosses told me that I would never have passed a security check in the United States, because I was a "premature anti-fascist," having started trying to join up before we went to war. I had no idea at the time why anyone would single me out to punish me for that.

I realize now that I was as glamorous to them as they were to me. Gaunt and nervous, aesthetically pleasing in the fashion that pleases at a given time, an object of interest, I had had the experience and touched the war they had come to share. But they saw as singular my joining the great majority in uniform. What I had learned to take for granted, service in the forces, was, to them, a fascination. It made them seem somehow younger than I was. I had a sense of knowing things. Oh, not events—civilians seem always to expect those—but gray expanses and hours, days, months of damp indifference. They didn't quite know what to do with me.

Three days after I arrived, I was taken to dinner at a black-market restaurant by actors so famous then that I was struck stupid. Burgess Meredith, a wonderful pixie of a man, had made a great success on Broadway, my old, abandoned ambition. Paul Douglas was one of those Hollywood "stars" who played the kind of solid, dependable man your parents wished you would marry. Both of them were in the film division of the OWI. They decided I needed feeding.

Where we went I still don't know. We were driven through dark, unfamiliar streets by one of those London cabbies who seemed to find his way like a night animal, with only the tiny slits of blue light showing from the masked headlights that gave no light to drive by but only warned pedestrians. And oncoming cabs.

We walked into an overpowering smell of food, a luxury of clean, white tablecloths and damask napkins from "before the war," which had already become a magic time, dimmed and changed by nostalgia. I remember that the room was dim with low, intimate lights, and the discreet cavelike atmosphere of London restaurants that used to imitate old libraries or men's clubs, with their leather banquettes along dark wood-paneled walls. In the corner, Jack Kriendler, from New York's 21 Club, sat with a foreign correspondent I have forgotten.

It was the only black-market restaurant I ever saw in London. People who knew each other had turned it into a home away from home where they had the comfort of being with their own in that network of fame I had hardly known existed. There they sat—correspondents, actors, Hollywood writers who had been trained to write too quickly from first impressions and would write about the war in the same way, a deadline war. Many a hungry GI slogged through mines in such meeting places, or the Ritz Bar, while the professionals and the shallow had no idea that they were missing everything about the war but the events.

My escorts treated me as if I were bone china. They ordered for me with great care. They were sweet, gentle, but unwise. I had been living on wartime rations, only two-thirds of that issued to men in the forces, on the military premise that women were smaller and needed less food, when I often towered over dole-fed Cockney men. I had stood naked in an FFI (free from infection) examination in a queue with a hundred draftees from the East End of London who had older bodies than mine would ever be from the bad food they had eaten. We were even a different color—pink with health or white with a sunless, deprived past. When I read in *War and Peace* how different the dead were on the battlefield at Borodino, I cried, because I had been there and remembered.

I can still see the plate of food, and smell it. A lamb chop, two inches thick; a baked potato with two weeks' ration of butter melting on it; and green beans. The smell of melting fat, rich meat, clean linen, and candle wax made my gorge rise. I prayed to get to the ladies' room in time, a prayer answered by seconds. The rest of the glamorous evening was spent with their taking turns holding my head over the loo while I was violently and repeatedly sick with dry heaves.

After that, I learned to face carefully both the food and the new aura of fame. I did it by returning to a refuge, a place in the middle between lorry and limousine, that I had found when I had come to London on sick leave to look for a job in late November of 1943.

To me, the place where I found comfort beyond imagination was in the clean, pale green, wonderfully civilian, genteel bedroom that Mrs. Doreen Green "let" through the offices of the English-Speaking Union. It was one of those nests of threadbare gentility that had survived all over Kensington, with ladies clinging to them, literally, for their dear lives, measured not in coffee spoons but in patched linen, polished tables, and the eking out of rations in bone china.

When Doreen Green had put her name on the ESU's very careful list of rooms, she said they had assured her that they would send somebody nice. I was the nice person she received into the citadel of her flat, on the top floor of a small apartment house in Kensington within walking distance of the Gloucester Road Tube Station, her first and last tenant.

So I had climbed the five flights of stairs and knocked at the door. The woman who answered it was of a subspecies of English women with careful accents who had dropped their wombs and their knickers for England in many far-flung outposts of the Empire. They could be recognized by their badly tailored, mildly butt-sprung tweed skirts and their oatmeal-colored cardigans. What saved Mrs. Green, though, was that she was more than English. She was Anglo-Irish, which gave her the strength of a sense of humor and a sustaining view of life, even of the war.

Her soul clung to the safety of a country house outside of Dublin called Ballawly, to which she went in spirit in time of crisis, trouble, or deprivation. Her living room, threadbare with war, with its fine eighteenth-century furniture that she kept explaining was from "Ballawly outside of Dublin, my family home," was as much luxury as I could bear. I found, in the country gentility and its habits to which Mrs. Green clung for sanity in the civilian war, a perfect kindness between the forces I had left and the luxurious raffishness with which I worked and played at the Office of War Information.

There the foreign correspondents, the celebrated visitors, the people who became my colleagues honestly thought they were living austere wartime lives. The entertainers, the people in the OWI, the film divisions, some of the foreign correspondents existed, without knowing it, within a caul of privilege they took for granted. It was not safety; they had come to a city where they could be killed, and many of them had come, as I had, in convoy. But their London, to me, was unreal, a stage on which a play called *the war*, in "a theater of war," was running. What impressed me most at first was the fact that they seemed to be able to call cars at any time of day or night.

Even the uniforms some of them wore were like costumes— well cut, no grease marks, no inground dirt, no fading or scratching, no ill-fitting crotch crease—in short, not the issue I was still used to. Most of them had no experience of the strictures in which Londoners lived, of being caught by raids late at night so that they had to sleep where they could. They did not have to step over the outflung arms of families who had slept in the tube stations for nearly four years. Once, in uniform, I had been caught in Piccadilly Tube Station by a raid, but in this new time I trailed my evening skirts along the narrow track between the sprawled people and the trains. I remember how innocent they looked, asleep.

Those who ate in restaurants had no inkling of what it was like to live on rationing, on scrounged, unrationed food, fish, or carbohydrates that meant standing in queues hour after hour, gray-faced with fatigue. One time I was in a taxi with a woman, made innocent by vast money rather than fame. When she spotted a queue at the horsemeat shop in Paddington, she said, "Isn't it amazing that those people still keep pets?"

So as soon as I got to London I went back to Gloucester Place to Doreen Green. She had managed to let me know, without mentioning it, that she had some money. She said that only her "wartime duty" made her even *consider* taking a lodger. She did, after all, have income, but it was, "you know, my dear," in trust.

She lived there with her fifteen-year-old son, Desmond, and one of those ancient splay-footed nannies who seemed a fixture in such families, left there after the children were grown. So I moved my trunk from Carlton House Terrace, tipped the butler properly, as a simulated major should, and hung my civilian clothes in my cupboard in the genteel pastel bedroom with its embroidered runner, its pale rugs, and its Victorian china knickknacks, all the fragility of the genteel poor.

She had told me the first time I went there that she was divorced from a husband who had lived too long in France when he was young and had picked up beastly habits from "those people." She confessed, as she ran her fingers over the beautifully nanny-patched runner on the chest in my new room, that when he had touched her *there*, she had no choice but to divorce him.

If London had become drab and shabby, flats like this one

were threadbare instead; *shabby* has an air of neglect about it, but *threadbare* is worn down with care, with meticulous patching, with make-do and make-do.

There was something of this in Doreen's small, pinched face, too, as if she would make do through the war as the others did, because she had to, and because the times were overwhelming except in the safety of the Irish antique furniture she had there, all that was left for her of what had been, at least in memory, that great Anglo-Irish country house. As with all of us, her safety was more psychic than real, since the flat was on the vulnerable top floor.

From time to time, several evenings a week in the winter, she gave us tea when I was there. I would bring home Mars bars, which she and Desmond loved, and she would slice them into pieces and serve them on china so thin I could see the shadow of her fingers holding it. Sometimes, too, we had sherry, one glass each; every time she held hers up, she looked through it at the lamp, and said, almost to herself, "The queen's physician advised me to take this every day."

Sometimes before she went on night duty in the Air Raid Precaution (ARP) she sat primly, dressed in her ARP uniform, ready to remain alert through the night, a woman too frail, it seemed, to survive an ordinary day. I can still see her hand, her wrist too thin for her ill-fitting uniform sleeve, holding a bone-china cup or a sherry glass. It was women like her, now forgotten in the more dramatic events of the war, who sat, night after night, on watch in the ARP stations, middle-class soldiers dim with worry that their homes would not be there when they went off duty.

During the nights of the "little blitz," when the air-raid warning sounded, we would gather in the tiny living room of the neighbors' flat on the ground floor and pretend not to be afraid. The ancient nanny, who seemed as much of a fixture in Doreen's flat as the dear antiques, the careworn and beautifully patched linen, would say, as the ack-ack guns in Hyde Park shook the house, "Is that one of theirs?"

Dutifully, Desmond or his mother would answer, "No, Nanny, it's one of ours." That Christmas, an ice storm turned the trees in Hyde Park into a glittering parody of Christmas trees. The children picked up from the streets strips of silver foil, which had been dropped by German aircraft to confuse our radar, and took them home to decorate their own trees.

At night, once in a while, if the sky was clear, a German plane got through the defenses of the city, and Desmond and I would run to the roof to see it, a tiny bug pinned in the sky by the searchlights that converged on it. After the war, I was told by an ex-Luftwaffe pilot that they were sent over London alone as punishment. Sometimes in the distance we saw sudden fires, as if someone had lit a bright flambeau in the black city.

When the buzz bombs began, Doreen insisted that Desmond and I move to the basement to sleep. She refused for herself; she said she wanted to protect her furniture. "Besides," she added once, "this is nothing to the Dublin troubles in 1916. You should have seen Dublin during the troubles. You could see the fires all the way from Ballawly."

So teenage Desmond and I slept on cots on opposite sides of a room that contained a large pile of coal, each of us with a blackout lamp to help us find our way to bed. The first night we went down, our neighbors teased us. Desmond, his little candlelit face serene, answered, "We are the WISE virgins." I slunk along behind him, not saying a word.

For Desmond, the basement was a new world. He thought I was the most glamorous creature in the world. When I came back late from dinner, I would crawl through the basement window like Peter Pan, sometimes dragging an evening skirt across the sill; he would look up from reading Proust by candlelight and ask me, as his mother would have done, if I had enjoyed myself. Like Scheherazade, I told tales, sometimes of famous movie actors, sometimes great poets, sometimes movers and shakers. Some of the stories were true.

Desmond would put down his volume of *Á la recherche du temps perdu*, from which he was learning French, blow out his light, and go to sleep.

At first, I was used at OWI as a courier to take VIPs to the BBC for interviews. Accidentally, I was plunged literally from lorry to limousine, from the barracks to tea at the Savoy with Robert Sherwood, Alfred Lunt, and Lynn Fontanne. I took Irving Berlin to the BBC, and he, with a capacity for friendship I have seen in few other people, made friends. He was tiny in uniform, too old already to be there; he moved like a cricket, doing everything anyone asked him to do. He treated others with a sense of rare peerage, as if it were the norm for people, and he was the kindest and also the funniest person I met in all the time I was escorting VIPs. He had brought over *This Is the Army* to play for the troops. One evening, we were to meet for a drink at Claridge's, and he was late. He came rushing in, apologizing as he ran, and sat down at the table. Then he said:

I have just had one of the most embarrassing days of my life. You know, we take *The Army* around to the hospitals. We have a small show, just the leads, designed so that we don't need a stage. Then I go with two or three of the singers around the wards to entertain the men who can't make it to the performance. There are some wards where they are too badly wounded even for that.

The commanding officer was taking me around to them, where I always said a few words, hoping to cheer them up a little. I noticed that we kept passing one ward. I asked why, and he said that the men were too badly off. I bounced in anyway. I told him that if they were conscious, I was sure a few words from home would help a little. It was too late to stop me.

There they lay, and I started my little speech about how proud we were of them, what brave men, all that. Usually, even from the very sick, I got some reaction. From these none. So I laid it on a bit thicker. I told them how proud their country was of them, how I represented their parents and their sweethearts to tell them we honored them as great Americans. I got no reaction at all. In the hall, I said, "What is the matter with those men? They don't react at all."

The commanding officer said, "I tried to tell you, Mr. Berlin. That was the VD ward."

Eric Hawkins, the editor of the *Paris Herald Tribune*, was a legend. Most of the twenties writers who lived in Paris had written stories for his paper that kept them alive through the thin years of beginning to write. One day he cracked open my door and looked in to find me typing, with the same two fingers I do today, my antiwar novel, which I later lost in a taxi. I think I started it because I was surrounded by real writers and had drifted into beginning to believe my label.

He said, "I know who your grandfather was. William Blake."

Then he disappeared as quickly as he had appeared. With that flying introduction, he set out to make me learn to work, and I will always be grateful to him for forcing me into a post-

Mary Lee (center) and friends Nida Tomlin (left) and Nicky Gockley (right) bid farewell to Sweet Briar College in Virginia with beer and cigarettes. June 1938.

2. *The Dunce Boy*, Barter Theatre, July 1938. From working with professional actors like Nell Harrison, Mary Lee learned discipline that would help her later as a writer.

3 and 4. While she searched in vain for acting jobs in New York City, in 1938 and 1939, Mary Lee supported herself by modeling.

5. The Rodney Weathersbees in the Settles' living room in late 1939. At Rachel Settle's insistence, Mary Lee brought her new husband home for a proper wedding in Charleston, West Virginia.

6. Lieutenant Rodney Weathersbee, on weekend leave, with his son Christopher. Toronto, 1941.

7. After Rodney was sent overseas in the fall of 1941, Mary Lee returned with Christopher to her parents' home in Charleston.

8. While her daughter was in England, serving in the Women's Auxiliary Air Force of the RAF, Rachel Settle raised Christopher in her "showplace" house in Charleston.

9. Grandfather Ed Settle joined the child-rearing effort with the help of the stray dog Christopher named "Company."

10. Most of Mary Lee's thirteen months in the WAAF were spent at Hullavington Air Station, where she worked in its tower (far left) as a ground-to-air signals operator. Photographed in November 2006.

11. The Savoy Hotel became the favorite gathering place for Mary Lee and many of the VIPs and writers she met through her work at the U.S. Army Office of War Information in London, 1944.

12. When she found this photograph of Christopher, age four, in a Christmas package, Mary Lee flew back across the Atlantic to reclaim her son.

13. After her divorce from Rodney Weathersbee, Mary Lee and the poet Douglas "Den" Newton were married in 1946. Here Mary Lee is wearing the famous suit she wore for all formal occasions throughout the years of poverty.

14. Desmond Green, the boy who shared basement sleeping quarters with Mary Lee during the "little blitz," later joined the RAF and lived with the Newtons on and off for ten years.

15. Den Newton, the sculptor Eduardo Paolozzi, Christopher, and Mary Lee, 1953. Christopher is wearing the "Sunday suit" and tie required of all the boys at Bryanston, his boarding school.

16. After the acceptance of her novel *The Love Eaters*, Mary Lee posed for this publicity photograph in the British Museum.

17. Mary Lee, London correspondent for *Flair* magazine, at home in Well Walk, London, 1950. The angel on the wall (at far left) would travel with her throughout the next fifty years to her last house on Decca Lane in Charlottesville, Virginia.

18. Columnist and historian William Littleton "Widdy" Tazewell, age forty-six, and Mary Lee, sixty, at their wedding reception in Charlottesville, Virginia, September 2, 1978. Over the next twenty years, they would enjoy a stable, fun-filled, and companionable marriage until his death from emphysema in 1998.

19. Between work sessions for her memoir, *Learning to Fly*, Mary Lee relaxes at a party given by friends in Kinsale, Virginia, February 2004.

graduate course in journalism when I was hardly qualified for the first grade.

On another day, soon after I began to work for him, he stuck his head in the door and said, "Hey, kid, have you ever heard of the Grand Coulee Dam?" I said no.

"Well, you better find out about it. I want five thousand words by next Tuesday." He scared me so much that I still remember facts about the Grand Coulee Dam I would rather forget. I had never written anything five thousand words long and never had faced that new term that meant so much—a *deadline*.

He sent me to the British Museum, which had been bombed and where the readers were relegated to a small back room. The great Reading Room with its glass dome had been damaged. I sat down at one of the long desks and began to learn to use the greatest library in the world. It was my first visit to a place that would be my Aladdin's cave for years and where later I would research and write *O Beulah Land*.

Almost imperceptibly, London moved out of winter and into a drab spring. The weather was cold, the days were gray, and there was a sense of watching the sky, as a farmer watches it, to read the future.

In the first preparations for the invasion, troops from all over the world gathered on leave in the West End of London. Cries for taxis and women in all their languages were plaintive in the blackout. Small, dim, blue lights, the only color allowed, read Bar, Pub, Restaurant. When the blackout curtains, hung like labyrinths at the doors, were pushed aside, we were met by a wall of light and noise and the uniforms, by that year, of all the Allies.

Sometimes there were mistakes. The Tivoli Bar at the Ritz had all the elegance and aloofness of yet another London club.

It was the home away from home for a mixture of the kind of Americans who knew about the Ritz, Guards officers, and assorted English ladies with what Hilaire Belloc called "loud and strident voices." Outside, in Piccadilly, it had the same small, dim, blue sign as all the rest.

Two American officers, new to the darkness of the streets, had picked up two girls from among the hundreds who haunted the West End. They had seen only the word *Bar*, and they pushed aside the blackout curtains and escorted the girls into one of the most exclusive venues in London.

The two girls had worked a long time in the streets. One's teeth were snaggled, the other had dirt scratched down her bare legs. Their clothes were filthy. It was obvious, but only for a second, that the two young men were actually seeing them for the first time. There was hardly a pause. They showed them to a table, pulled back their chairs, and followed the perfect Chesterfieldian advice, "Treat the duchess like a whore and the whore like a duchess." Not a word was said by the waiter, who entered into the scene with all the arrogant politeness he would have shown any other customer. I was never prouder of my countrymen than I was then, when they, far more insouciant than the British around them, soothed the feelings of a pair of embarrassed Piccadilly whores.

The OWI crowd met in bars and restaurants and turned them into havens. There was no place else to go. Nobody seemed to have a home. The Petit Club Français had more movie actors, ballerinas, and American writers than the Free French for whom it had been opened. The long front room at the Connaught, which looks like a comfortable drawing room, gathered the OWI, the foreign correspondents, and, often, the most fashionable of London's poets. There were scores of places, all over London, where people found their own.

I had not yet found a haven. I had been flung from group to group at first. I remember Claud Cockburn, who wrote for *The Daily Worker* as Frank Pitcairn. I lent him ten pounds when he ran out of money one night in the back bar of the Café Royal. He paid me back with ten shares of the *Week,* a Communist broadsheet he published every week with all the lowlife "capitalist" intrigues he could find in either the British or the American government. It earned me a black dossier as a part-owner of a Communist magazine. I was fascinated with all of this, with the paradox of a mixture of secrecy as a flirtation and of naive hope among most of the intelligent people I met then.

It was on that night in the Café Royal that I found out about the three-way Spanish Civil War that I had heard of as a rumor, and about which George Orwell wrote *Homage to Catalonia.* I introduced Claud Cockburn to Arthur Lehning, one of the Middle European scholars who worked for "black radio" in Dean Street, where the OWI broadcast to the undergrounds in Europe.

Arthur Lehning was the most middle Middle European I knew. He looked like it; he spoke like it. I had never known real academic brilliance before, and I have seldom seen it since. He had been the director of the International Institute of Social History in Amsterdam when the Germans marched into Holland. He had changed his reading glasses for his distance glasses, put on his black hat, and dressed in his formal clothes; he had then packed a suitcase, walked down to the docks, hired a rowboat, and proceeded to row out to sea.

He was picked up by an English destroyer that landed him in (I will guess) Southampton. He borrowed some English money, took the train to Oxford, walked into the Bodleian Library at Oxford University, and asked to speak to G. D. H. Cole, one of Oxford's most popular historians. He was told that Professor Cole was not available.

He placed the suitcase on the reception desk, and said, "Will you please keep this in a safe place until after the war?"

"What is in it?" he was asked, of course.

"The whole of the Marx-Engels correspondence," he replied.

So this was the man I decided to question. I asked him if he had been in Spain during the civil war, and he said no, that he had left just before war broke out. With the usual post-adolescent twenties cynical sneer, I asked why. He answered, "I shot the Archbishop of Saragossa."

When I looked shocked, he explained, "He was not in Saragossa when I shot him. He was in Madrid." Lehning told me that he had been a Syndicalist Anarchist.

It was then that I had my chance to find out about the three-way war. When Claud Cockburn came over to our table, I introduced them. "You were both in Spain," I said, putting the cat among the pigeons. Claud Cockburn, Communist, had been in Madrid. Arthur Lehning, Syndicalist Anarchist, had been in Barcelona.

About two hours later, they ran down after accusing each other of losing Spain.

I had lunch, through Cockburn, in the Ivy, one of London's fashionable restaurants, with the editor of The Daily Worker and a Communist deputy from Belgium. I asked him when he had become a Communist.

He answered, "When I was fifty, my dear. It was not, with me, a youthful error."

Maybe I was being recruited, I don't know, and I wasn't interested. I was young and full of curiosity. I was far too curious, too questioning, and, by then, far too experienced at being a pawn to blind authority to be attracted to dictatorship, proletarian or otherwise. Only a few months earlier, I had been ordered to run along behind a proletarian sergeant who was as mean as a snake, as she rode her bicycle through an RAF station. I am still, this many years later, outraged that I didn't pull her off her bicycle and blacken both of her little squinty eyes.

I sat on the stairs in Mayfair at a ball in one of the grand houses in Grosvenor Street with a pink Guards officer, nineteen years old. Looking with some disdain at the people dancing, he said, "I'm frightfully sorry you see us like this. Before the war, half these people would not have been invited."

I said, "Before the war, I would probably not have been invited." When I visited his parents at Longleat, one of the most beautiful houses in Wiltshire, he asked me if I would like to go for a walk. I said yes. We hiked for miles without a word, and when we turned to go back to the house, he did a perfect Guards military turn. He had just left Officers' Training School. He was killed in the invasion.

In those days, we talked as people have not talked in England since. We talked on trains, in bars, in canteens, in Lyons Corner Houses, on buses, as if our statements had to be made before it was too late.

I often walked in Hyde Park with Archibald MacLeish. I remember one day in early spring when the pale sun seemed to bless us. The daffodils and mimosa from the Scilly Isles had just that day arrived in London; they were the yearly harbingers of spring. He had been shocked because he had taken armfuls of flowers to the editor of the *New Statesman*, and his wife had thrown them on the hall table and forgotten to put them in water. This seemed to trouble him, as things did then, when everything around us was so changed and we found, from time to time, little evidences that there was some continuity that had nothing to do with war. We talked about that, and the flowers from the Scilly Isles, and how *Anabasis*, the long poem by Saint-John Perse, translated from French into English by T. S. Eliot, had influenced the writing of his own epic poem, *Conquistador*. Both of them are still favorites of mine.

On one of our walks he told me that he had spent the rest of his life finding out that what he knew at eighteen was true. Years later, I would test this by writing *The Clam Shell* about my own eighteenth year.

An OSS (Office of Strategic Services) officer from Hollywood tried to convince me that I must be a Communist. "But you do recognize the historic inevitability, don't you?"

He sounded annoyed. The joke was then that the OSS and MI5 spent more time following each other and all of us than they spent watching German spies.

I sat on the wall by Hyde Park Gate, across from the statue of Boadicea, with a young American fighter pilot who flew P-38s. He had just been posted to a station in the south of England. On the way through New York on leave, he had seen a wonderful new musical, and he sang to me, "Oh, what a beautiful morning."

It was the first song I ever heard from *Oklahoma*. He was killed the next week. His parents sent me a letter thanking me because he had written to them that he had enjoyed our day. I never wrote back. I didn't know what to say.

In one of those decisions that seemed to have been made for the sake of decision itself, I had been moved down to the radio section in Dean Street, Soho, broadcasting studios for "black radio," beamed at the Resistance in Europe. I wondered, then, if people were really risking their lives to listen to an essay on the Grand Coulee Dam or the music of Aaron Copland.

Dear, sweet Marc Blitzstein, the author of Orson Welles's production *The Cradle Will Rock*, composer, lyricist, naive GI, sat with me in a room as we chose records for the mobile propaganda trucks to play loudly as they drove toward the German border. Kurt Weill and Mozart, Blitzstein and Wagner—we chose them all to be played until the truck stopped and an American voice called out over a loud speaker, "Surrender!"

Ironically Blitzstein's most successful production was his translation and production of the German composer Kurt Weill's *Die Dreigroschenoper* (*The Threepenny Opera*). He told me the story of how he began to translate it. He had tried for several years to get Weill to change his mind and give him permission to translate it and produce it, but he never succeeded.

"Then," he told me, "a miracle happened. I was coming back from Kurt's funeral when, almost as if Kurt were telling me, the first English words for *The Threepenny Opera* just sang their way into my head." He never knew he was being ironic. After the war, Marc put Lillian Hellman's *The Little Foxes* to music in his opera *Regina*. On the island of Martinique, he was murdered by three sailors in a homophobic hate crime.

For several years, the painted words of rain-soaked graffiti ran down the walls all over London, saying, OPEN THE SECOND FRONT NOW. By mid-May, the days of double daylight saving time were so long that we seemed always to be walking from morning to twilight under a solid blanket of American and English bombers stretched across the sky all the way to the horizon. During the short night they flew on, never stopping the roar above our heads.

Some of the men I worked with, and the correspondents, became edgier and edgier, drank more, caroused more, fell into silences. If there had been not a single spy in London, the world would have known from the poised waiting, the departure from London of troops, that at last, what we all called "the second front" was going to be opened. Then, for forty-eight hours, day and night in early June, the loud drone of the planes over-head never ceased. One morning, I got up at dawn after a sleep-less, drone-filled night and walked down to the radio station. The only other person there was sitting in her office and watch-ing the wall. When I asked what was happening, she snapped, "None of your business. Shut up."

For some reason I still can't fathom, she had been let in on the secret, and she was sitting there vicariously invading Europe. It was the morning of June 6, 1944.

Everything changed that day. London woke up; the pace was faster. I was assigned to the midnight briefings at the Min-istry of Information in the London University building. They seemed futile, since correspondents and troops were coming back and forth in an open corridor that made London seem like a part of the front itself.

Then, on June 13, in the middle of the night, the first buzz bomb flew over London, the engine cut, and it crashed into a mews, killing six people.

It was the first of Hitler's long-rumored secret weapons. They came—self-propelling, unmanned bombs with little stubby wings. They looked like huge cigars and sounded like motorcycles in the air. Some were shot down coming over the coast; more came into London. We began to listen; we listened all the time, whether consciously or not, for the cutoff of the engine, which meant that the buzz bomb would either crash straight down or glide.

One night, when Desmond and I were sleeping in the base-ment, we were awakened by a buzz bomb roaring overhead. Then the engine stopped.

We waited, each in our dark corner.

It seemed more minutes than it was when the bomb

dropped a hundred yards away. The building only shook. Then there was silence.

Desmond's voice came from his corner: "Mary Lee, if that sort of thing happens again, you mustn't run over to me and I mustn't run over to you, because if we were found that way, mother would never understand."

Desmond Green was to become one of the best friends I had in the world until his death fifty years later.

Everyone thought his or her own part of London received the brunt of the buzz bombs, and there were rumors about which targets had been chosen. Nothing was chosen. They fell completely indiscriminately, ludicrously. I went home to Gloucester Terrace one evening to find Doreen sobbing. One of her friends a few streets away had been wiped out, with her whole family, an hour earlier. She kept saying, "They were only getting ready to go to the theater," as if that had anything to do with their useless deaths.

The next day, I walked down with her to see the damage. The Air Raid Precaution crew was still digging in the trash heap redolent of dust and plaster that had been their home. I pulled her away and made her go back to the flat and put sugar in her tea. Usually she would pretend she didn't like sugar so that Desmond and Nanny could have more of the meager ration. She had confided in me that she drank her tea with lots of sugar for energy when she was on duty, since it wasn't rationed at the ARP station. Somehow the memory of teatime with her, and the death in the other house, seem linked together, as they should be.

I was on a train coming in from a grand weekend in Wiltshire. There were many of them, those weekends even when I was still in uniform. I think those hosts and hostesses made me their war work: a countess near the RAF station; nearer London, Lady Astor, whom I found horribly familiar as a Virginia female tyrant; and several members of the widespread Astor clan, who were wonderful to me in London. They included one of England's best comedians, whom I was to see long after I had faded away from the others into peace and another life.

Sitting across the carriage from me was an unattractive, shy young Jewish refugee from Germany who had been conscripted into the Pioneer Corps. We began to talk. When he began to talk about music, his face took on a glow. He invited me to a Prom concert at Royal Albert Hall. We climbed up to the cheapest seats just below the great round glass roof.

Away in the distance, a tiny figure, Myra Hess, played to the kind of silence she commanded from the huge crowd. She was playing a Hindemith cadenza to a sonata by Mozart when a buzz bomb rode over the hall. We could see its faint shadow through the dirty glass. The pure, small sound of the music was the focus of a dead silence. Her fingers never faltered. We were hypnotized by her concentration, and the bomb exploded a hundred yards away, across Kensington High Street in Kensington Gardens. She had kept us from a panic that could have killed many people. It was the last concert there until after the war.

Often there was no way to get home from the midnight briefings. So late at night, after the last tube, I sometimes stayed in the bomb shelter at the Ministry of Information. One evening after the briefing, Gene Solo, a scriptwriter from Hollywood attached to the OWI film division, said, "Don't sleep here. We all have a room at the Savoy and a car. Come with us."

I said I would go if I could have a quart of milk to drink. When I got there, a table had been drawn up between two twin beds. Dixie Tighe, William Saroyan, Gene Solo, Irwin Shaw, and a man from *Newsweek* were playing poker. The game seemed to have been going on for some days. I lay down behind the safe, broad backs of Solo and Saroyan, drank my two weeks' ration of milk in a room that reeked of gin and cigarettes, and went to sleep deeply for the first time since the buzz bombs had started. I was awakened in the morning by Irwin Shaw, throwing pound notes in the air and yelling, "I've won! I've won!"

What made for a sense of safety so often was not true safety at all, but rather a psychic calm—Doreen Green sitting among her dear Irish antiques on the top floor of a London building. I finally had found my own psychic safety, my own home away from home. I went like a pigeon to the cote to the top floor of a building whose walls were a twenties decor of small glass mirrors that would have shattered into a million shards if we had been hit. But I had found my pub, my local, the kind of place you go to unthinkingly, the place that becomes habit almost as soon as you see it. No place else had done this until I had met another refugee in the corridors of the OWI. We made friends as quickly as children.

He was the most ridiculous GI I have seen. Chinless, pop-eyed, hair cut by Trumpers, already and impressively a published poet in his early twenties, newly graduated from Harvard, where he had been a protégé of Robert Hilliard, Dunstan Thompson made even the ill-fitting GI uniform of a private soldier look elegant. Someone had rescued him from the more useless assignment he would have been given in the army, as I had been rescued. That is, if some drunken GIs had not hit him over the head one dark night to serve notice to a proudly and openly gay man, who fortunately lived on until 1975.

He already knew every "literary" first name in London. When I told him I was working in the OWI as a writer, he accepted me completely as what I was trying to be. He was already used to people who wrote and published, rather than those who still only wanted to do so, or those who posed. I think it was this, and his acerbic kindness as a natural teacher, that made me really begin to write—not as a caprice or a lie but as a dedication I have never lost. He also made me realize how ignorant I was, so I began to read contemporary work and classics, filling a great hunger like someone who has been starving and doesn't know it.

I had had only one teacher before who had opened that haunting and frightening possibility. It was Joseph Dexter Bennett at Sweet Briar, who had guided me to a clutch of small books he had brought back from London for the college library. Now those poets, Stephen Spender, C. Day Lewis, George Barker, were real; they had names, and drank at the Gargoyle Club, and ate their jugged hare. And there were evenings when Dylan Thomas was sitting on somebody's knee; when Robert Newton broke things; calls sounded across the floor to Cyril and Stephen and Guy; boyfriends quarreled in the men's room; and a woman who passed as valid because she had once been the mistress of a poet whose name I have forgotten was sick on the floor of the ladies' room.

I was having lunch at the club with two journalists from Belgium when a buzz bomb stopped overhead. No one else stopped eating. The Belgians, who were not fools, took one look at the glass walls and dove under the table. I suspect that everyone else wanted to, but there was a kind of foolish noblesse oblige, and one was to sit upright when the buzz bombs halted overhead so as not to disturb the others. One feared more than anything else showing fear or being caught cringing. Social fear was far and away more powerful than personal panic.

I had moved back to Carlos Place when the news was pouring in day after day. There seemed to be some attempt, not at political censorship but at not disturbing the American people with more than they could take. How long did it take us all to realize that we were no longer fighting a conventional war? We were in an invasion of hell run by efficient clerks.

On the beaches of Normandy the Allied armies met such an international army of conscripts that they had to comb London for people who spoke obscure European (and other) dialects and languages. There were even two Tibetan prisoners of war.

Marc Blitzstein and I continued to sit in an office, choosing records from American composers to play on the loudspeaker systems of trucks when they were not calling for the Germans to surrender. The war was running down, and we knew it was nearly over. There was some naive hope that things would be "better" than they had been before the war.

The Beveridge Plan for social services had been debated in Parliament in an all-night session during which Quentin Hogg, one of the "young Turk" Tories, had brought the members to their feet cheering at his words: "If you do not give the people social reform, they will give you social revolution!" This, at least, was a shout in the right direction, but when I asked another member about it, he said, "Oh, we always cheer when somebody uses two political clichés in the same sentence." The Labour Party was getting its slate ready for the first postwar election, and when I asked Harold Laski whom they were choosing, he answered in his little pinched professional voice, "We [the imperial "we"] have decided on one-third workers with the hands, and two-thirds workers with the mind." Lovely Kay Kendall sang, "I'm going to get lit up when the lights go on in London," and we all cried.

John Armstrong, the painter, asked me, as a "young person"—when I was as old that day as I will be until I die—"What do you young people hope society will do after the war?"

"I, for one, have no communal hope," I told him, "only recognition that individuals must become just, before the world becomes just. John Keats defined *just government* as the government with the most just men. That belief is all that is left to me."

"If I thought that, I would commit suicide," he told me. He was an older, sweet left-winger whom I was ashamed to hurt, with his hope retained as romantically as Doreen Green's "before the war" in Ireland.

On September 8, I was walking with a friend in Soho when the ground under us heaved and then was still again. We thought it was a small earthquake. Fourteen miles away, the first V-2 had landed in Chiswick. In some vague attempt to keep knowledge of the hit from the Germans, the news was released that a gas main had exploded in Chiswick. For a while, the V-2s were called "flying gas mains." They were terrible, in all the classic sense of that misused word. There was no warning. If you heard the explosion, you were safe. They killed hundreds more people than the V-1s had done, and, unlike the buzz bombs, which sounded like great bees in the air above London, they were entirely without sound.

I had had to take a room near the office during the crisis of the invasion—as if where I lived could possibly affect the outcome. One evening, I was sitting in a tub of hot water, trying, frankly, to get warm. London's damp cold seemed to have seeped into my soul that night.

In one second, I heard almost next to my ear an explosion unlike any I had heard before. It was as if the open sky had smashed. The water from the bathtub flew out onto the floor. Then I knew what real freezing was, the freezing of total fear. I knew that one of the V-2s had landed near the square. My sane mind realized that, having heard it at all, I was safe. The V-2 in fact had landed in Pimlico, roughly a mile away.

The "hell weapons" for the "efficient clerks" had changed the face of the future. They came on their own, as impersonal as lightning strikes. They were without any target but the city itself—machines without planning, without anger, just killing machines, so efficient that Wernher von Braun, their inventor, was taken to the United States as a trophy. They were the forerunners of the modern missiles we are dropping on cities so that troops won't have to "go in," the modern synonym for invasion.

It was a miracle that the V-2s were not launched earlier. I believe that London could have panicked under too long a siege of them.

This is the first time I have faced consciously and recorded that moment in a bathtub almost sixty years ago. It has made me realize that I have been reliving the terrible shock of that noise ever since. It used to be called *shell shock*. Now it is called *post-traumatic stress disorder*. I have always thought it was the signals shock caused by fatigue and enemy jamming; now I have experienced far more consciously, by writing this, that the climax was a V-2 that only knocked the water out of the bathtub. That has made me react to surprise or even faint noise by reliving with a faint scream the residual shock from which I still suffer with neurotic hearing.

It is not the strike but the terrible noise that must leave such residual fears among so many in cities that have had "precision" bombing. It started for the Middle East so long ago, in Mosul, in what is now Iraq, with the first bombing from the air on any city. When the British bombed that city as part of a "pacification" after the defeat of the Ottoman Empire, the

Arabs watching from the countryside said that the British were cowards to fight from the air instead of coming down and facing their enemies like men.

I put some of those words in quotes because they were invented for the actions they define. In the depths of my being, I knew and still know that I had heard the coming of a brave new world. Yeats, in "The Second Coming," asked, ". . . what rough beast, its hour come round at last, / Slouches towards Bethlehem to be born?"

I know now that that three-year stint was the central event of my life. I can never again judge with the destructive innocence of class or intelligence. One is a fortress, to me, a prison. The other is a gift. To those, now from the experience of three wars, it is more than a memory, it is a reliving; those who suffered it, in the biblical sense of going through it, wear it in their soul. It is not an illness to be overcome. It is an honor to the others, not to forget them. When your grandfather suddenly talks about it—which he seldom does, knowing that it is not transmittable—pay attention. It is not trauma; it is not "post-traumatic stress disorder." More often than not, he is sharing with you the center of his life.

I had the first conscious experience of this reliving when I traveled to England with my son and a friend who had also served as a Red Cross volunteer in England and France. It was the fiftieth anniversary of the end of World War II. I had been asked to write about it.

We were on our way to the tiny village of Stanton St. Quintin, where I had been billeted in a country house. I asked to be let off on the main road so that I could walk alone the mile or so that I had walked every day or night to and from the Flying Control Room.

I was only a few yards down the familiar road when I realized that I was marching, not walking, that my arms were at an angle, that my stride was a military stride. A (then) seventy-six-year-old woman had become a twenty-three-year-old WAAF again, a body responding to recall, and living within it.

8

LEAVING

❧

One day in late December, I received a parcel from my family. I remember nothing that was in it except a photograph, one of those posed, framed, and retouched. It was of Christopher, the first they had sent me. I looked at it, went straight to Eric Hawkins, and asked to be transferred to the OWI in New York. He asked why. I showed him the picture and began to cry.

By early January, he had arranged for me to fly home. I gave up my room, said goodbye to all around, including Doreen and Desmond Green, and was put in a room in the Connaught to wait for the right weather for the Pan American Airlines plane to cross the Atlantic.

But the weather took time to improve, so I stayed in vast luxury in the Connaught, across from the OWI, for three weeks. Suddenly everything was calling for me to come home. Within that three weeks, I was told by a dear friend from Richmond, Virginia, that Rodney's father was having me followed so that Rodney could sue for divorce, naming a correspondent so that he could claim damages under English law, since the wife was the property of her husband. I laughed about it. I knew I was being followed, but I thought it was either the OSS (predecessor of the CIA) or MI5, its British equivalent; everybody was following everybody.

I went to a fashionable solicitor, the English name for a lawyer, which I found odd under the circumstances. He had been suggested by friends as the best for divorces. I put it in his hands and instructed him to tell Rodney's father's solicitor that we would countersue, since the property (me) would not be damaged but vastly improved. I had yet to find a correspondent, but I had offers.

I was in my solicitor's office when he called the opposition, representing Rodney's father, and said, in answer to a question, "No. It was her idea. I can do nothing with her. She is an American."

I was not too concerned. I knew that Rodney—who at that point was fighting with a Canadian commando regiment in France and had been slightly wounded and returned to service—had other concerns. I also was certain that he would never have sunk to such greedy action. It was never his way. Neither of us, thank God, was vindictive.

Both of our parents, on the other hand, were to behave as if Christopher were a rubber ball to be thrown between them. I had him made a ward in Chancery on the advice of Lance Beales, who became his "first friend," lovely legal language for a guardian. It meant that Christopher's future could not be decided in a lower court.

The next thing that happened during that three weeks was that my mother sent a letter to Senator Chapman Revercomb of West Virginia, a friend, saying that she had a heart condition and needed me at home. This, too, arrived on the London desk. Everything was conspiring to lead me back home.

Finally we were given permission to fly. I have forgotten where in England we went to board the plane, but I can never forget the plane itself, or what turned into a wild and comic crossing of the Atlantic Ocean. It was my first by air, and the first for most of the people on the plane.

The two-engine propeller plane rested on pontoons in the water of a harbor I have forgotten; we were handed down into it from a dock. The interior was well-upholstered, subtle pink in color, and in peacetime it had been a luxury plane for carrying passengers to and from Central and South America. If the flight were overnight, it turned into a sleeper, much like the old Pullman cars on trains, but pinker and grander.

The first stop was to be Shannon Airport in Ireland. The plane was tossed through the windy sky across the Irish Sea. I was not sick, but some were. By the time we got to Shannon, the weather had closed in again. We were grounded.

We were driven by bus to an inn near the airport. The village of Adare was beautiful, which tells nothing about it. We sat that night, all strangers, in an ancient Irish inn, in front of a peat fire, drank Irish whiskey, and I think began to realize, each of us privately, that we were out of the bombing. One of the passengers was the Dutch diplomatic courier, with the diplomatic pouch locked to his arm. Another was a red-faced, tight-collared businessman from London. There were two men—one from the Foreign Office, one American diplomat—who decided that I needed taking care of, and several other nationalities I don't remember.

Relief, warmth from the fire, and the Irish whiskey made us friends. It was like a shipboard friendship that fades as soon as the destination shore is reached. Outside, the wind blew and the rain beat on the inn windows. We got happier and ever more contented until the Dutch courier passed out.

The American and the Englishman decided that they would both put the courier and his pouch to bed, so that they could watch each other to see that no security was breached. They staggered up the two-hundred-year-old stairs, propping up the courier and his locked pouch, and disappeared into the darkness.

The next day, it was still damp and the sky was low. A light Irish mist made the ivy-covered ruins of the monastery or castle, I can't remember which, look romantic. Some of us climbed the snaggled stone ruins. Finally, on the third day, we were cleared to fly to Lisbon.

That day it snowed in Lisbon for the first time in seventy years—only a light blanket that disappeared in a day, but it was enough to ground us again. We were taken to a white wooden hotel. Its porch of nineteenth-century fretwork designs led to wide steps down onto the street. The pavement, as far as we could see, was a long, wide path of *azulejos* tiles in huge, bright floral patterns.

Half-hidden in the trees lining the sides of the road were lights that cast shadows across the mosaic. In the early evening, when we got there, the lights had just been turned on. It was the first time in three years for me, four years for most of the passengers, that we had seen such grace and color, the mosaic pavement illuminated and the electric green of trees, instead of the unforgiving darkness of the blackout.

I walked down the steps beside the red-faced English businessman, who reminded me of Rodney's father. When I turned to look at him, the tears were flowing down his face.

We were grounded for two days in Lisbon. By that time, we were on holiday as well as we could be. The purser for Pan American Airways, a Portuguese man who looked like the twin of Tyrone Power and spoke three languages, kept us quiet by taking us around that beautiful city during the day. Lisbon had been almost entirely destroyed in the mid-eighteenth century by a huge earthquake, and her rebuilding had made it famous as a model city.

The town squares were mosaics of *azulejos* in bright colors—blossoms, leaves, abstract designs, tangled vines. One was paved with blue, green, and white tiles laid as waves of the sea, so the paving seemed to move before our eyes. Another was abstract, with patterns I would learn later were influenced by the long-ago Muslim period in Portugal, as was the making of the tiles themselves.

They are gone now. The automobile has won, and a huge Sheraton hotel has been built in the place of the fine white wooden one from the early nineteenth century.

The street beyond it is no longer tiled. When I was there a few years ago, only I, and one old man who worked at the hotel, had even known about the color and the magic. But the hotel manager, who was twenty-nine years old, was excited to find out about it and was planning to revive the memory of the old hotel and the street with pictures in the new lobby.

That January evening, our group was taken to the casino, one of the most famous in Europe, at Estoril. Portugal was neutral during the war, so Estoril had become a haven for spies, nationals from other countries, expatriates who didn't want to leave.

There were clutches of people—French, German, English, American—around the huge roulette table, with spaces between them as if formally they had mapped their territory and honored the enemy.

In what once had been a grand room, the red velvet draperies hung neglected and stained. There were worn foot-paths across the carpets. Even neutrality had not saved Estoril from the damp neglect that is the setting of war.

On the third day, we flew to Africa, down its west coast

where the world below us was divided into yellow, sandy land and blue sea, as defined as if it were a drawn map. We were to put down at Dakar to refuel and prepare for the third leg of the journey, the crossing of the Atlantic at its narrowest point between Africa and South America. This narrower route had also been chosen for the slave trade to America.

Bubonic plague had broken out in Dakar, so we were not grounded but quarantined. Passengers were allowed ashore only as far as the government customs and landing buildings. A few of us chose not to go at all.

We were assured by the pilot and copilot that we would fly on the same night, and that we would not be grounded; the weather looked fine, and so on. It was, I remember, about three o'clock in the afternoon. After the pilot had gone along the aisle to speak to the few passengers who were left aboard, he stopped at my seat and leaned over. He asked me if I would like to see inside the cockpit.

Of course I wondered if he were making a pass at me, the Atlantic crossing version of "Come up to my place." Pass or no pass, I, of course, jumped at the chance. The controls looked as functional as the Wellington bomber I had already seen, known as the Wimpy for J. Wellington Wimpy, of comic-strip fame.

As we turned, he probably to begin the formal pass, I to go back to my seat, I saw the "met chart"—the meteorological chart. I must have squealed in panic, "We're not going to fly through THAT, are we?" I pointed to a five-thousand-foot front in mid-Atlantic. He jumped in front of the met table. He was furious.

"You should have told me you could read a met chart," he said.

"You didn't ask me," I informed him, settling down to do

some hard blackmail. Two of the sleeping bunks had been prepared so that the pilot or copilot could rest during the flight.
So, safe behind the pink curtain, having swallowed two of the
pilot's sleeping pills, I passed out on my first of so many flights
across the Atlantic.

The next stop was the most magical place I have ever seen.
We put down at the mouth of the Amazon, at Belem, in a
charming Brazilian government compound built against the
background of the Amazon jungle. In the sea beyond us, our
plane was a small seabird riding the blue waves.

Of course we were placed, once again and on the same day
in late afternoon, on the kind of dozing porch that I was beginning to recognize as delightful nineteenth-century colonial
architecture, the center of life, facing a garden, the jungle
around it, and a quietness interrupted only by the cries of birds.

There we were given *cuba libres* and, with the same good
manners, escorted one at a time to have our temperatures taken.
Then we were put into cars and driven to what was little more
than a clearing in the jungle. It was a town square, and nothing
in it had been built later than the late nineteenth century.

There in the jungle was an opera house, with life-size
carved figures leaning over the entrance, staring with their
marble eyes at the jungle. There was a town hall that matched
it, and a beautiful small hotel with complicated, frail-seeming
wood carving.

This was Belem in 1945; since the Allies had been cut off
from the Far Eastern rubber trade, this little lost jungle-
covered city had been dug out, awakened like a sleeping
princess, reclaimed, and repainted.

It had all the easy charm of a dream of the past, when
Belem had been a boom town, where fortunes were made in
rubber, before it all failed and disappeared under the choking

vines and massive trees of the Amazon jungle. We stayed at the little hotel that night—it, too, dug out and brought back to life for the new seekers-after-rubber.

We did not see the wartime installations. I don't remember the new raw ground cleared for the export of rubber to the Allies. I only remember flying within sight of the great river, and staying in that clearing of a preserved nineteenth-century town square.

Those who had cleared the town had left—behind a high steel fence—a tiny jungle to remind them that it was ready to take over if the place were ever abandoned again. I wonder if that little fenced-in jungle still exists. I suspect not.

Now Belem is one of the largest ports in South America, with a fine university and skyscrapers that rise into the equatorial sun, but I never want to go there. My Belem is a fairy tale, and that's the way I want to remember it.

After our flight across the jungle and over the Caribbean the next day, we put down at a little bit of England at war. We wouldn't have known that, however, from the welcome we got there.

We sat waiting, yet again, but this time within the main room of the port duty and immigration building. Or so it seemed. Nobody explained. The dazzling white uniforms of the Royal Navy were everywhere. This would be our only glimpse of the island of Trinidad, BWI, or British West Indies. Without unseemly showing of it, this was the southwest corner of the battle of the western Atlantic. British warships and those camouflaged Q boats—tankers and cargo ships, preferably old and down-at-the-heels, which were secret warships[1]—patrolled the western Atlantic and the Caribbean rim for German U-boats.

---

[1] Q ships, or Q boats, were attack vessels disguised as civilian ships. They were used in World War I primarily by the British and in World War II primarily by the United States, which officially ended its Q-ship patrols in 1943.—AHF.

These young men in their whites, who were being so polite to us, escorted us, two by two, into the privacy of a room where we had our temperatures taken. It was done as casually as if we were taking our turn at the loos. As soon as we had finished, we were asked, if I remember correctly, how we would like our rum. I think we stayed the night in a hotel surrounded by a huge garden in Port of Spain, but all I remember is strolling that night under the stars in a garden somewhere in Trinidad with a young man in whites of the Royal Navy.

Years later, my husband and I did go back to Trinidad, and I learned more of where I had been. The Atlantic on the western end of its smaller sister island, Tobago, plunged almost straight down to the abyssal depths of the sea, and the fish, smaller in the coves, were huge. One of the plantations that were left had been turned into a small hotel; we stayed there and wandered where a young English couple in the mid-nineteenth century had been caught by yellow fever and buried in a tiny formal cemetery, all that was left of their short life there.

After our tour of more of the world than we had expected, when we were full of peace and sun and good food, our luxury plane, which had turned the crossing into a cruise, set down on the water by a dock on the island of Puerto Rico. There we were told to wait, fifty-two of us, side by side, on two long benches. Fifty-two thermometers were shoved into fifty-two mouths and we sat mute, trying not to giggle, until they were collected. Our passports were examined. We had technically entered the United States. Only we hadn't. There must have been fifty more passengers crowded aboard from Puerto Rico en route to LaGuardia Airport, some of them standing.

So, tired of surprise, tired of flying, tired of war, and in a daze of relief, we watched the Clipper put down at the sea entrance to the new LaGuardia air terminal, in its final landing on Atlantic waters. The trip had taken eight days. For me, for most of us, the war was over.

We were herded into a room even before we had gone through immigration and customs. I did not recognize the uniform of the man who leaned against a table and lectured us on security. He informed people who had come from Europe that there was a war on, that loose lips could sink ships, and finally he let us go to line up at what I remember as a steel gate, where we gave our names to a man standing with a notebook in his hands.

My turn came, and I said, "Mary Lee Settle."

"We know all about you," he told me, and I was allowed back into my country. I found the remark ominous, and, still searching my mind for what he might have meant—the imperial "we," the look—I took my turn at customs. Finally I walked, still flanked by my protectors, into the huge, round lobby of the new LaGuardia Airport.

A man in a black overcoat, a black homburg, and a blue and white polka-dot scarf around his neck rushed up to me. "Jane, Jane," he yelled. "Thank God you've come back to me."

That he was crazy was obvious, and that he was dangerous was obvious, too. His Jane had come back and, come hell or high water, he was bound to rescue her. My escorts pushed him away, and we rushed toward the bus that was to take us into Manhattan. In the distance, I could still hear him calling, "Jane! Jane!"

The airport authorities put him on our bus to be turned over to the police, I suppose, at the Pan American terminal in the city. He sat in front of me and, turned around, he told me and my bus mates, all the way into New York, the whole history of our love. It was pathetic. It was also, after all the travel, irresistibly comical.

The driver stopped the bus somewhere in uptown Manhattan to let out one of the passengers. When he left the bus to get the baggage, my polka-dot lover slipped into the driver's seat and actually started the bus to take Jane home with him. The driver and two men managed to collar him.

At the Pan American terminal, we ran across the floor and out into Forty-second Street, and I was rushed into a taxi. One of my friends told the driver to take me to the Algonquin Hotel.

I spent the next day doing the most sensible thing I have ever done. In the morning, after a wild night's sleep, I took myself to Elizabeth Arden, where I went through the all-day rest, petting, haircut, facial, and massage. There was another woman just ahead of me in the series of luxuries. Never once that I could see did she look at anybody or speak. She was taken through like an automaton. When she sat facing a mirror, her eyes were dead; she did not look at her own face. I was told that she had just arrived from a Japanese prison camp.

That evening, I was invited to Constantin Alajalov's studio apartment for dinner. He was one of the cover artists for *The New Yorker*, and somehow, during the prewar summer, we had become friends through that network of Europeans who worked in New York.

It was my second night back from war. My dinner companions were Alajalov, Tilly Losch, and an elegant Free French officer who had been sent in his beautifully cut uniform with his beautifully cut aristocratic face as a propaganda visitor. Recognizing that we Americans love a lord, it was his assignment to improve the image of the country that had been occupied since

1941, and to obscure the truth that so many of its citizens had collaborated with Hitler, or been passive, under the Vichy regime.

He said at dinner, taking for granted in the company that it was an acceptable remark, "Well, at least Hitler did one thing for us. He got rid of the Jews in France."

I was too frozen with shock to move or speak. I felt drained of life. Despair can leave you too lost to resist seduction. The thing I had not known about, that war can do, I found out in that moment. You go along. I did not leave quickly enough. In short, I was polite. I have been ashamed of that ever since.

But that moment, casual to them, has left me with something, when I think of it, like a darkness of soul, and recognition of the waste of the dead, the years of deprivation, of grayness, of dedicated uselessness. It has thrown the responsibility straight onto a society in any country that Turgenev called "the rich, the happy, and the unjust."

It has taken me a long time since that night to realize that the war years were not wasted. I have had to face the fact that social change does not change evil people. There is only this difference. Their seduction is no longer officially tolerated in democracies. Evil men and evil prejudices are with us still; those of them who are "nice" people belong to anti-Semitic country clubs, and their imitators drive pickup trucks with gun racks and hate "niggers." The only thing that saves us is that such beliefs have been unacceptable to decent people since 1945. I know that *unacceptable* is a small word for this enormity, but the world runs on shallowness for the most part. We are left, at least, with a residue of social shame as a weapon.

9

THE TURNING YEAR

⌒⌣

This was the year that struck a chord within me of such urgency that I have listened for it and lived by it ever since. It has been the sound of my work, my life, my decisions, and often my defeat, but it leads, this pied piper, along a straight and narrow road.

It had started in London in December of 1944, but I could not define a way to go; it was like the fire alarm in the night, the demand for movement. Its strength has guided me through decision, not too deeply scarred, beyond my *patria chica*, as the Spanish call it, their "little homeland."

I went down to my parents. Christopher and I greeted each other almost as if I had not left, but that took a few days. When I got off the plane, he hid behind my father.

We were going to live in New York while I worked in the New York office of the OWI. I found a place to live, a sublet of a furnished railroad flat on Fifty-second Street just beyond Third Avenue, in the building that, later, wonderful Judy Holliday entered to shoot her husband in the film *Adam's Rib*.

A few months after the dinner at Alajalov's, I was sitting in my office at the OWI when someone walked in with an armload of photographs. They were the first pictures from the Bergen-

Belsen concentration camp, which had been liberated on April 15. My job was not political. It was not aesthetic. It was simply to find out how much I could take of what I was seeing, an emotional censorship. The pictures passed through my nerves and my eyes, the faces, the great eyes. Some made my stomach turn and my eyes glisten so I couldn't see.

After a few days, I asked to be relieved of the job. I admitted that the images were affecting me less and less. There was an armor of brute dullness that I had grown to protect myself. Maybe. "Getting used to" something like that can be a terrible defeat.

Because there had been the memory of so much false prop-aganda in World War I—babies on bayonets, raped nuns—some people in London refused to believe their eyes. One of them was the Conservative MP who had been so kind to me when I went to Cliveden. She insisted on joining a group of MPs to inspect Buchenwald. When she went home, she put her head in the gas oven.

There were more suicides after V-E Day, as the day of Germany's surrender was known. The familiar pictures of people shouting with joy and relief and kissing strangers in the street have been shown ever since, over and over. But the suicides were not mentioned. One was the U.S. ambassador to England, John Winant, known as "Gil," who stayed in London all through the war. He was the most beloved of the Americans who were there. His tall, Lincoln-like, slightly awkward figure was well known; he had made it his business to go to bombed-out areas to offer help. He had, for me and for all the others who worked in the section of which Grosvenor Square was the center, an unforgettable sweetness.

For those of us who had come back to New York, the relief of realizing that we were safe turned terrible, and I still don't know why. It was not the city; it was ourselves. The beginning of peace was like a torn nerve for us.

One day I went to a matinee on Lexington Avenue. The movie was *Meet Me in St. Louis.* Between showings, there was a short called *V One.* I paid little attention. Of course I knew it was about the buzz bombs and the rockets that came after them, but I had lived through them with the same insouciance that was demanded of all of us. But when the loud, airborne-motorcycle noise that started the film ripped through the dark theater, I collapsed and had to be taken out into the lobby by first-aid people. When I could sit up and then stagger to my feet, I assured them that I was fine so that I could get away from them.

My apartment was just around the corner on Fifty-second Street. I managed to get the door open, collapsed on a sofa, and cried for as long as it took for the day to turn to electric night. This many years later, I have to stop my day's writing. At eighty-five, I am still too upset to revisit any more.

A dear friend, whom I had known before the war, was one of the most meticulously groomed young American officers in London. He was attached to headquarters as an adjutant to an American general. One day, when I had been in New York for several months, there was a knock at the door. It was he, still in uniform, with several days' growth of beard, dirty. His clothes looked as if he had rolled in a gutter. All he said was, "Let me in and don't say anything."

I went to my cousin's wedding. She was marrying a newly returned young officer. It was, everybody was saying, a lovely wedding. To me it was obscene; they were all so pink, so plump, so dumb, so healthy. There were parties and music and little shrieks of southern delight. There I met a strange-looking young man who had just returned.

He said little until he found out that I, too, had come back from the war. Then, in the middle of all the party noises, in a low voice, he told me that he had been liberated from Buchenwald concentration camp, where he had been taken after being captured. His B-24 Liberator had been shot down. He had followed the directions for escaping France by contacting the Free French Resistance. They had begun to pass him from one cell to another, and one of the cells had been infiltrated by a Nazi, who turned him over to the Germans. Because he was caught in civilian clothes, he was not treated as a prisoner of war. "At Buchenwald they didn't even hate us. It was indifference." *Indifference* was his term for the experience—along with a vow to kill the man who had betrayed him and others. Several American pilots were rescued when Buchenwald was liberated.

He had gone in weighing one hundred eighty pounds, an ex-football player. He came out weighing eighty pounds. His strange look came from his quick gain in weight, which made him seem swollen.

When the atom bombs were dropped on Hiroshima and Nagasaki, he flew to New York. He surprised me by arriving at my apartment, sobbing. All he could say was, "Not this way. Not this way." Then he got drunk.

These were not great events. They were our reactions, all different, but through them ran a hot wire of anxiety, still there with many of us, really to be triggered by circumstances or surprise. We simply could not stand peace, and there was nobody to discuss it with but each other. What we had brought back with us—even I, whose corner of the war was so small—was an inability to live on the surface anymore. It no longer held us up. My memory of that summer of 1945 is fragmentary; the connections are gone, as in remembering a dream. How the scenes changed. Vivid without connection. I have tried to define it, but

the memory is fragmentary, although it was defined by so
many around us. I remember a friend making a sexy joke of it
by lunging at a returning soldier and saying, "Come here, baby,
let me rehabilitate you." It was not their fault, the pretty girls,
the worried parents. It was not ours. Easy definition diminishes
this time into events.

When war seemed to have ended, and New York was in a
riot of celebration, I was working at *Harper's Bazaar*. Frances
MacFadden, from *Harper's Bazaar*, had been one of my mentors
and friends at the OWI in London. It was she who, without my
knowing it, had recommended me to Carmel Snow, the
Bazaar's famous editor-in-chief.

Christopher was with me at home. I had found a very nice
housekeeper who came by the day, a European refugee who at
least seemed to know a language we could speak. Christopher
went to a day school where he had playmates. On one of the
days when I visited the school, they were doing a play. All the
children were dressed in costume. Christopher was a rabbit. He
hated it and was terrified of the audience of noisy, gushing parents, who I am sure thought they ought to be joyful, gushing
parents. Maybe that was it. Suddenly, what was expected of us
was not what had been expected of us in the war. The social
clothes differed. There was so much we did not say. Those
events of what they thought of as war were neither war nor
peace, movie imitations. How could they know? It would take
me twenty-five years to try to define it.

I remember sitting through a *Harper's Bazaar* editorial
meeting where they, not I, were deciding whether the obliga-
tory Bergen-Belsen pictures—I recognized them and said
nothing—should be printed before or after the French hats.
The joy of peace was that when Paris was liberated, Christian
Dior turned style into a cure for all the make-do that had

gone before. (Could I believe they talked of it as "the fashion world"?) His designs were taking the world by storm in a teacup.

Everything for me moved so swiftly that I can only remember it in scenes, and in attitudes that I found repugnant among the innocent. One of the attitudes, and the worst, was an aesthetic view of the war. Jim Agee sat huddled on a little ottoman in my living room and showed a picture he had cut from either *Time* or *Newsweek*. It was of a German cadaver on the battlefield, his hair flung back along the ground. He looked like Siegfried, the beautiful blond beast, sleeping. He was an adolescent boy who seemed untouched by death.

"Isn't that beautiful?" Agee said, passing it around a circle of friends I had made too quickly, handed out of kindness from one person in London to another in New York. I was an oddity; I had been to war. I wanted to be sick, but I was not. I was getting used to being there among those whose concern was so unlike my own. Alice Morris, who worked at *Harper's Bazaar*, was Harvey Breit's wife. Through them, I met most of the writers who were in New York. There were a few with whom I felt at home, could speak, be serious, and be understood. One of them was Dwight Macdonald, another was Niccolo Tucci. But every day there were the fashions and the women with taut faces who had looked at my body in expensive clothes and not my face when I had been a model.

The day before my birthday was a Saturday. Christopher was visiting my parents. I had gone into the office to do some work when nobody else was there. I had found it hard to concentrate. It was a mist-laden day. I could barely see the details of the Empire State Building, fifteen blocks directly south of my office. It seemed to float, a ghost of itself, in the air.

Silently as I watched—I must have been looking up from

my work to think—a huge black hole seemed to grow slowly on the side of the building. I thought I was hallucinating. It was only when I went home that I found that an airplane had hit it. There had been no noise.

The fall came. Christopher and I sat at the breakfast table in the kitchen, which we had made into the center of our lives. He said, "I like you." I said, "I like you, too." This boy, this barely five-year-old boy said, in grown-up fashion, "I didn't think I was going to. I was afraid." I waited, knowing not to speak. "When I did anything bad, Mommy and Daddy told me it was the Mary Lee coming out in me, like a sore. I thought it was like that."

That was how I found out that they had taught him to call them Mommy and Daddy. I know that they were innocent of wrongdoing. We all have so many unquestioned habits, such armor of innocence.

"Autumn in New York." The song is true. The memory of the breeze, the hurry, the blue sky, the new beginnings, was everywhere, and I was part of it, marching up Madison Avenue in my best disguise. In a hat, in my dependable Bianca Mosca uniform, with the right jewel, the white gloves, I strode up Madison Avenue toward Voisin for lunch with the editor of *Vogue* and two of her assistants. They were courting me to move to *Vogue*. All I remember of the lunch was that everybody was well dressed and the dessert caddy was three tiers high.

This is about a single moment and a voice. I have told it before and will again, the voice, the moment. I have had few such moments, but I have known them, what they were, how they demanded. I went back to my desk at *Harper's Bazaar*. On it were layouts of the Bill Brandt photographs of Brontë country—Haworth parsonage where the sisters had lived, the Yorkshire moors where Cathy had run with Heathcliff, that greatest dark lover in literature. Brandt had caught the wind, the darkness, the wild, haunting, demanding moor that brooded over the story. Alexey Brodovitch was the art editor of the magazine, one of the best, and he gave me such material for captions.

Beside the layouts lay a copy of *Wuthering Heights*, with a biographical introduction. I began to read it. Emily Brontë had written the book and was dead by the time she was thirty. I was already twenty-seven and had done nothing but flirt with a vocation and earn my living as one of those who fattened on such work. I knew, as clearly as I remember now, that I had to choose, and that I would not have such a revelation again. I knew at that minute that I was being blessed, no other word. Me in my hat and my red fingernails, an undeserved blessing, for no blessing is deserved or earned. It is only granted.

So I threw my hat down on the Yorkshire moors. I marched into Carmel Snow's office before I lost my nerve and chose a sensible course. I told her secretary that I had to see Mrs. Snow urgently.

She sat at her desk, that successful raddled face, that self-demanding chic.

I said, "I quit."

Carmel Snow's face muscles had not shown surprise for some years. They didn't then. She simply said, "What do you want to do?"

I found myself saying, "I want to go back to England where everybody is as tired as I am."

"All right, my dear, I will have you transferred to the *Bazaar* in London." That was all. She looked down at some papers on her desk and I said, "Thank you."

She did her part in my life as casually as she would have assigned me to a story.

∾

The furnished apartment was in the right part of Kensington, my postwar clothes were hung up, the friends had gathered. I had entered into Literary London from Literary New York—one who wrote about it, not it. Cyril Connolly, the mentor of taste, art, philosophy, and food at the time, gave me advice after I sent him a short story. "You are a novelist," he told me, as he sat on my floor eating caviar that the New York store had sent by mistake when I had asked for a monthly food parcel to augment the rationing for Christopher.

Then he ate several more tins of caviar from Christopher's CARE parcel and talked about how unhappy he had been as a fat boy at Eton on scholarship.

I was being set up as one of those American ladies who came to London as soon as the war was over to flog careers and give parties. Christopher was kicked out of Miss Puttock's school for young gentlemen. (None of the gentlemen was over five years old.) She said, "All the other children take off their caps, put them on the assigned peg, and say, 'Good morning, Miss Puttock.' Your child throws his cap at the peg and says, 'Hi ya, Miss Puttock.' The others are beginning to copy him."

Now the last day of this turning year—not of the year itself but of my changes within it—came on a fine Saturday afternoon. One of the people who had reappeared was Douglas Newton, whom I had met in Cambridge at the house of Lancelot Beale and his wife. We had stood on a bridge across the Cam and talked a while, leaning on the railing and watching the punts slide by below us. He called that day to invite me to a concert at Wigmore Hall. I said I couldn't go, that I was busy.

So I sat in the back of a limousine dressed up to go to one of the first grand weddings at St. Margaret's Westminster—the daughter of the Duchess of Grafton or some such. There were, and perhaps still are, people in London who don't think their marriages are legal unless they marry from St. Margaret's. Why I was invited I don't know. I don't remember anything else about the ride toward St. Margaret's. I only know that I reached forward, tapped on the glass between the driver and me, and said, "Take me to Wigmore Hall."

After the concert, Douglas Newton (called "Den"), Michael Tippett, one of England's leading young composers, and I walked down Wigmore Street on the way to an Indian restaurant they called "The Glory Hole." The food was terrible, and cheap. Michael was wearing my white gloves over his ears and Den was wearing my hat.

PART II

THE APPRENTICESHIP

When Mary Lee cast her lot with Douglas "Den" Newton, she entered a new world, or, as she puts it in the title of the following chapter, "another country" within the metropolitan area of London. It was very different from the glamorous, socially connected, Literary London she had come to know in 1944 and returned to in the fall of 1945. It required a monastic commitment to "uncompromised" writing—nothing short of the finest work that one was capable of doing, regardless of literary fads or market demands.

For nine long years, she would soldier on, filling drawer after drawer with manuscripts of short stories, plays, and at least three novels without publishing a single thing except the journalistic pieces she wrote to buy the time for her serious work.

During those years, she and Den and her son, Christopher, traveled back and forth from London to the West Country of England, sometimes thumbing their way to various retreats in Cornwall, then Essex, until, finally, in the early 1950s, they settled into a six-story house in Chelsea and rented out all but three rooms.

All the while, Mary Lee was continuing to write, day after day, year after year—in bed when she was ill in their Camden Town apartment, then in work rooms set up in a barn in Mevagissey, Cornwall, in the summer, and in a house in Well Walk, where she and Den were caretakers. During one relatively flush year, they had a lovely house in Bardfield, Essex, until the loss of income from Mary Lee's job as "English correspondent" for *Flair* magazine drove them back to London to set up the communal house in Sloane Court West, Chelsea.

The story of those peripatetic and impoverished—but intellectually luxurious—years from 1946 to 1955 in England is told in the next chapter. It appears to be the last chapter of *Learning to Fly* on which Mary Lee worked, accessing it on her computer on February 23, 2005, when she was recovering from radiation treatment just outside of Charlottesville, Virginia.

The five pieces that follow it: "Mr. Eliot," "Coronation," "Nine Years," "Maugham," and "My Paris" have been taken virtually "as is" from the same computer. She had grouped them there with the finished chapters of *Learning to Fly*, intending to include them and, probably, hoping to have time later to work them seamlessly into the memoir.

The fragments, "Nine Years" and "Coronation," are new text that she drafted in June and October of 2004, respectively.[1] The other three chapters, "Mr. Eliot," "Maugham," and "My Paris," are polished essays written in the 1980s for publication elsewhere but clearly central to the story of the fledgling writer.

Like the first chapter in Part II, the final chapter, "My Paris," is a compression of experiences over several years—in this case, trips to Paris between 1949 and 1954. Rather than try to pinpoint exact dates, the reader should instead relax and

---

[1] This was a particularly hectic time in Mary Lee Settle's life, and it is not hard to understand why the two fragments were left on the computer to be completed or worked into the main text later. In June 2004, when she started "Coronation," she was getting ready for the move from Kinsale to Ivy, just outside of Charlottesville, Virginia, making lists of books and furniture to be packed and writing letters to secure funding for the coming year's research and the writing of a first draft of *Tom*—the project that had now become her first priority.

In the weeks before her eighty-sixth birthday in July, she was treated for a small skin cancer on her nose with a cream that seemed to cure it. But her health was clearly failing as she pushed on through the move to Ivy in August.

Although frequently short of cash at this point in her life, Mary Lee was never short of courage. In mid-August, still exhausted from the move, she ignored a fever and a racking cough long enough to give a brilliant speech on Thomas Jef-

enjoy the memories as they flow, free from constraint, through Mary Lee Settle's astonishing mind.

In the end, it is a special triumph for this southern girl who used to be ashamed of her intelligence that in learning to fly as a serious writer, she also learned to value and expand, and then share with the world, the extraordinary gift she had been given at birth.

—Anne Hobson Freeman

ferson in the garden at Monticello. It was, she said, "the best speech I have ever given." A few days later, she was in a hospital being treated for pneumonia.

Soon after she drafted the two pages of "Nine Years" in October, an X-ray and CAT scan revealed an inoperable small cell cancer on her left lung, and she began a regimen of chemotherapy and radiation treatments. From January 2005 until the time of her death in September, she would have to use an oxygen tank—about which she gamely quipped: "*All* writers need to be tethered to an oxygen tank. It keeps you from running away from your work!"

Her sense of humor never left her.

In the summer of 2005, as she lay flat on her back, she said she hoped to stay in that little house on Decca Lane until the very end because she was so grateful to the owners for renting it to her. "And don't you think it might increase the real estate value to be able to say, 'This was the house in which Mary Lee Settle died?' "

10

ANOTHER COUNTRY

❧

Three months later, on the night before Den and I were married, Conrad Aiken took us to a pub in Camden Town.[1] I had joined a little country within a city; it was not the Literary London of chasing the famous or making careers. If there was envy, and there was, it was outweighed by the daily fact that we had all chosen, or been chosen, to live as we did in order to work as we needed to. I had thought it was a choice. It wasn't.

It had been a crossroads, and many of those I knew took another way, the way of fashionably articulate London. That endlessly long tradition had stretched from the sixteenth-century School of Night with its contempt for Shakespeare, now known, if at all, only by literary scholars. In the eighteenth century, it had been the dictatorship of opinion by Doctor Johnson. And then there was the now-forgotten John Lockhart, editor of the *Edinburgh Review*, who is known now only by hav-

---

[1] Mary Lee Settle was married to Douglas "Den" Newton from 1946 until they were divorced in 1956. He was not only a poet but also an expert on primitive art, serving as curator and then director of the now-defunct Museum of Primitive Art in Manhattan, then chairman of the Museum of Primitive Art at the Metropolitan Museum of Art. Born in Malaysia and educated in England, he died at age eighty on September 19, 2001, in New York.—AHF.

ing given bad reviews to Emily Brontë and John Keats (he advised the chemist to go back to his pots).

I might have been seduced by the fashionably literary circles out of innocence, but Den, who had so keen an awareness of the often-praised shoddy, the on-the-make, the *claque*, despised literary games. To him they were imitations of true talent. Not who you knew but what you did were unspoken watchwords. He was educating me in courage and I did not, at the time, know it. He was the best-read person I have ever known, and also the most talented. But talent was two a penny. Everybody had it.

We had made friends with Conrad Aiken in the way we did in those days and among those people. We liked him and admired his work, and we invited him to our apartment in Camden Town. When he heard that we were going to marry, he insisted on giving us a party the night before.

So the three of us sat in the pub for hours, asking and telling, drinking, and, in Aiken's case, reminiscing with such ease and honesty that he has been a model for me ever since.

I asked him about his short story I thought was wonderful, and uncompromising, a word of Den's that rang with approval. It was "Silent Snow, Secret Snow." He laughed, and this is what he told us.

During the Depression, like everybody else, he had no money, and he realized that if he were to keep on living the way he had to as a poet—he said integrity was getting very expensive—he would have to write some prose. He had a dollar, that was all. So he went to the drugstore and bought three magazines—*Judge, Collier's,* and *The Saturday Evening Post.* He studied the stories they printed and paid well for, even making a graph for plot and character. He swore that he thought he had followed the unwritten rules of what sold. The result was "Silent Snow, Secret Snow," one of the finest of classic American short stories. "I guess I wasn't any good as a whore," he said.

But how many others of his generation had been and would be destroyed either by the self-demand for a "standard of fame" or by the habits of the "successful"? In another context, Jimmy Baldwin was to call it "knocking at the door of a burning house."

I was getting used to the fact that, without knowing it, I had made the right choice by returning to London. Money was not a constant temptation. Nobody had any. There was little to buy anyway, no seduction of things. If we wanted to drink, we went to the pub. If we wanted to go someplace, we went on the bus or the train or, as we were to do so often, to and from Cornwall by thumb. If I, who have had a weakness for fine clothes ever since my seduction by modeling them and being able to buy them at cost as a model, wanted clothes, either I or a friend made them from a sketch I drew.

Living in London was never, in my case, the longing-turned-to-imitation that seduced so many who went there just after the war. I had already lived too deeply among the English for that, for any romantic view. But I saw them, the constant graduate students, longing to be part of some magic they thought they could pick up by imitating lives and knowing people. Despair became a fashion; everybody half-read Kierkegaard, stopping before the *Concluding Unscientific Postscript*, which was like ending *Tess of the D'Urbervilles* with her walk down the nine-mile Roman road to Bridport in Dorset. Despair was a fashion and a fearsome weakness that haunted people, including me. I remember a friend, who had caught not the reality but the fashion, saying to me about a well-known literary hanger-on in London, "Darling, you would *adore* her. She's tried to commit suicide *three times*!"

There was a magic, and such despair was not part of it. It contained a healthy, demanding anger, a demand that was turned on oneself, the society, a healthy way of using the dark days. At one point Christopher said, almost in tears of disappointment, "The Angry Young Men are friends of my *mother*."

It began to spread among us all soon after the war, and we lived within it. We had survived, not in military terms but in keeping alive and now allowing to flourish the right to exist without regimentation.

One evening a group of us had been invited to take part in one of those arid discussions in a new gaggle of art groupies of the kind that sprang up in London to help the arts, as if that were possible in committee. We sat in the back row, duffle coat by duffle coat, trying to look angry and succeeding in looking grumpy, when one of the presiding poets, I think it was Stephen Spender, asked, "How do we know? How do we *really* know what we create is art?"

Eduardo Paolozzi lumbered to his feet and growled, "Either you've got it or you haven't got it." There was nothing more to say and we all went home.

There were three rooms in our apartment—one for Den to work in, one for me, and one for Christopher. He still says that those days in Camden Town were the happiest of his early years. Den was not "fatherly" to him; he simply treated him as an equal. If Christopher had a bad dream, Den took it seriously and discussed the matter.

One early morning, Christopher called out, "There is a tiger on the shed roof next door!" Instead of saying, "Go back to sleep. You're having a dream," Den got up and went into Christopher's room. Then he called me. It was not a tiger. It was an ocelot, one of the big cats from the zoo, which was within walking distance of our apartment. Den called the zoo and we watched them recapture the animal with nets and a hypodermic before some fool shot it. Christopher learned first from him the love and protection of animals. I see Den fleeing back to London in a third-class carriage with a dignified line of kittens sitting side by side with their paws tucked comfortably. They had been threatened by a local farmer who had accused them of stealing his eggs. The mother, Brit, scion of a thousand generations of Soho cats, sat beside them, her paws also tucked comfortably.

Our apartment was also the "address" of fourteen or fifteen conscientious-objector friends of Den, who were spread all over the south of England, on the run. The government had been too slow in releasing them from their assigned farm work when the war was over. When Den decided to report, expecting to go to jail, I remember ironing his one shirt, and crying. He came back an hour later and said he was off the hook. They weren't interested.

Michael Tippett often stayed with us. One morning he came into the kitchen and announced he had had the best night's sleep since leaving the Scrubs. The "Scrubs" was Wormwood Scrubs prison, where "conchies" served time for refusing to do even the war work of being field hands.

It was a delightful friend, one of the editors of the *Architectural Review*, who told me that when he was in Reading Jail, he learned that ever since Oscar Wilde had been there, they had had a prison cat named Wilde.

One day there was a knock at the door. When I opened it, there stood Desmond Green, looking pale and weedy in the uniform of the RAF, his little face under the jaunty cap of an

Airman Second Class. He had been "seconded" to the London University School of Languages to learn Turkish. As a child of the "officer class," he used the word "seconded" for transferring or posting. He had been given thirty shillings a week to find a place to live. He would live with us for much of the next ten years.

Christopher had his sixth birthday there, and we and our friends made it a memorable one. There was a puppet show. I made the theater and a friend carved Punch and Judy and the Policeman. My family sent glories of candy and cake and favors that had been unknown during the lifetime of most of the guests, who came from the houses and apartments of Camden Town. We decorated Desmond's room with streamers and color and a large tub for bobbing for apples. But it was the candy, which had been rationed through the lifetime of the six-year-olds, the candy canes hanging from streamers on the ceiling, the baskets of jelly beans, that struck them dumb, except for one little Cockney who breathed a long, awed, bird sound, "Cooooh."

There was a crisis. Christopher ran into the kitchen to tell our friend Judy Wogan, a diminutive actress who had once been known as the pocket Venus of Dublin, that we had forgotten the baby. There had to be a baby for Punch to throw out of the theater onto the floor.

Judy thought for a minute and then found a carrot in the vegetable bin. She carved the face of an angry baby on it, then dressed the carrot in bright tissue-paper clothes, with a ruff around the baby's neck. The puppet show was a huge success. Judy, the smallest of us, crouched behind the waist-high apron of the theater, spoke all the parts, and sang, "I care for nobody, no not I, and nobody cares for me!" The baby was flung out onto the floor; Punch was hit over the head by the Policeman's stick and taken to jail.

As soon as the show was over, the audience made a concerted plunge for the baby, and even though they had had enough food to founder them, and two had been sick from the unaccustomed feast, they passed the baby around and took ritual bites of it until it had disappeared.

Den and I decided that we would let Christopher decorate his own wall, as long as he didn't use the crayons anywhere else in the apartment. He still says, many years later, that at first he couldn't believe his luck after the awful tidiness of my parents' showplace house. So planes flew across the wall, and ships floated, and there were suns and moons and stick figures and animals and sunsets and just plain ecstatic streams of color. When he tired of the pictures, he came to us and said, as we had asked him to, that he was finished with those paintings and would like to make some more. Either Den or I whitewashed the wall, and he began again.

It was that wall that undid me. It was my turn to paint it, but this time when I squatted down to paint the baseboard, I froze there. I managed to lean sideways enough to rest on the floor. It was there, an hour later, that Den found me and helped me to bed. I stayed there for nearly a month, frozen in place. It was the beginning of what for most of us was the inevitable demand of our bodies and minds that we recognize profound changes in our lives.

One day, when I had begun to stagger to my feet, I was sitting in the kitchen with a friend from Washington, who had taken the trouble to find me. He turned on the tap to fill a kettle for tea. When I heard the sound of the water, I began to cry. What would be a lifelong weakness from signals shock was coming to the surface. I could not stand surprise noise of any kind. Instead of being shocked, he told me about a training called the Alexander Technique that would help me.

The people who taught it were founder F. M. Alexander's niece, Marjorie Barlow, and her husband, William Barlow, the only doctor who had given up an orthodox practice to teach it.

At first I hated the Alexander training. I found the people, who seemed to have formed a sort of club that demanded release and conscious ease, too self-satisfied, convinced they were right. All I wanted to do was to be left alone to cry my way out of endless trouble and sorrow.

Then, gradually, the training began to "take" in my body and mind. It was to give me a way of learning to use my energy so that I could bear the stress of that wartime permanent injury, and the choice of what is recognized to be the hardest work I will ever do. The fatigue of writing, the demand of concentration, not "being a writer" but actually writing at the same time, in the same place, day after day, year after year, has never been better recognized and explained than by Joseph Conrad, who wrote that he had loaded hundredweights of coal in the dead of winter from six in the morning to six in the evening when he was a sailor in Amsterdam. He said that the fatigue was nothing to a day's work of writing.

I have seen the crisis I faced happen to many sick people who have begun to learn the Alexander Technique. What residual illness or weakness brought them (and me) to it, as a last resort, surfaced and had to be faced. And I went through a time of illness when I was so pale with fatigue that I thought I was going to die. I could barely get up from the bed. I had to be helped even to the ignominy of the bathroom. It was, I realized when it was over, life-threatening fatigue, and it was suffered by so many of us who, instead of taking on the fashions of despair, were trying to shed it to prepare ourselves to do our work and live. The fact that Christopher existed was, I know, the final hope that pulled me through it and made me long for and learn health.

This fatigue had many names; mine was called peritonitis. I was kept in bed; when I tried to get up, I turned gray. Everybody came, sat around my bed since I couldn't get up, and carried on with the perpetual arguments that we all kept going. Christopher, at six, had to be sent to the "country" part of the Town and Country School, where he had been for two years.

That was the worst of the time, but he may have been better off in the country. At least there they could find fresh vegetables and eggs. In London it was, I found out later, the worst winter since the war—colder, less fuel, less food. Fatigue in all its names struck everywhere that winter.

It was decided that I would have a hysterectomy, the great sacrificial operation, as primitive as self-flagellation. I supposed it was to cut out the hysteria from my gut. All of this was well beyond my decision.

I was put into the hospital at Paddington, a historic building whose wards had been designed by Florence Nightingale and never changed. The ward I was in had a series of beds down either side of a hauntingly empty high ceiling and huge windows where the color of cold turned the ward into a gray mist, and the structures for curtains when someone was being examined or was dying looked like iron cages in space.

So I lay there reading Salvador Dali's autobiography, not the best for such a vast surreal room, and I was surprised to find that people I would never have expected came to see me. The visitors came in and out and carried on their interrupted conversations across my bed. That was how I found out how cold the winter was. They came to get warm.

The head nurse was a parody of dotty discipline. When I tumbled the bed covers while turning over, she ran to me, as she did to the others, straightened the sheets, and tucked them in like straitjackets. So we lay in white rows, staring at the vast ceiling, and when people died, the curtains were pulled around the bed, and sometimes there was the faint sound of prayers.

But I was having, inadvertently, what I had needed so desperately, a complete rest, so when the operation took place, the nurse told me that the surgeon had said, "There's nothing there." She said that since he already had me opened, he straightened a few tired muscles. On Valentine's Day, I made a valentine for the staff. I drew myself lying on the operating table, which of course I had never seen, since I was given ether before I was wheeled in. I drew a large heart, open on my belly; it was also an eye, à la Salvador Dali. The caption read, quoting the favorite film, "Here's looking at you, kid."

I still am a student of the Alexander Technique, and I still make an uncontrollable, almost-silent scream when I am surprised by noise. I have lived with a wartime disability and a means to control it ever since.

Why these stories? They bring back a time so valued. Sickness and health and the beginning of a lifetime of work, all together in that nearly empty cheap apartment in Camden Town. A plunge of local children. A son six and then seven years old. A group of friends who came to sit around my bed and take up discussions where they had left off, an illness taken for granted, since so many were reaching these crises, entirely unexpected, payment for the lives we had left, and the dangers we had faced. It was hard living.

It was also completely full living, both good and bad, for all of us. Yes, we stood in queue after queue for herrings (I knew at least ten ways to cook them). Yes, we were strictly rationed—so much so that when my parents began to send a monthly CARE parcel from Holland of eggs, cheese, frozen steaks, and butter, the unaccustomed food made us all sick. As a result, it had to be carefully rationed as well. The housewives of London looked as if they had stood in their queues for hours, and often they had. Life was a grapevine of where the fish and the vegetables could be found, the only unrationed food, and they, I, all of us, trudged day after day, pushing wire shopping carts like empty baby carriages. I called the queued-up, gray-faced women "the dropped-womb set." There was even a comic parody of us all in the *News Chronicle*, a column about "Brave Little Mrs. Ruby Gissick." We loved her. She could make a tin of sardines "go to four" by clever arranging of the plates for dinner. She helped us laugh at ourselves.

But with all that, I knew for the first time in my life that I was in the right place; in the words of Thoreau, "I was born in Concord, and just in the nick of time."

The scenes of that time come together as if it were one fine day in my memory. I see myself working every day on a big board propped on the bed. I stop by a chair in front of the gas fire. Time stopped. I stood there in a still center that I did not define or think about. When I moved again, nearly an hour had passed. It was my first experience of meditation, and waiting, the two most precious tools for writing. I have begun the day with that pause ever since, the clearing-away of all the tension and cacophony of daily life so that when and if work should come to me, I am prepared.

I lived among people who seemed to have read everything, who argued the merits of George Eliot's *Daniel Deronda* as easily as they did the latest literary success. I read and read and read; it became a habit I still have. The ones that guided me I still carry from country to country, house to house. There they are: Conrad, Hardy, Eliot, and Proust. We have come together to this room where I write, from those learning days in London, not what is to me the overstructured correctness of graduate studies but the wonderful excitement of discovery, of what was left with me and will be there until I die, the whole record, book after book, guide after guide. There were so many clues, so many teachers, but three above all stand out for me still: Conrad's introduction to *The Nigger of the "Narcissus,"* Proust's introduction to *Contre Sainte-Beuve*, the chapter in George Eliot's *Adam Bede* that begins, "This Rector of Broxton is little better than a pagan!"

Money? Den worked at a new magazine, *Contact*, whose editor had been one of the most famous editors of the *Architectural Review*. It was one of the now-failed magazines that would affect both content and layout for years to come.

As for me, my whole attitude toward work had changed so radically that it was a true conversion. I no longer worked to earn money, to be successful in terms of the world around me, to make a living, or to buy luxuries that all too easily could turn into necessities. I did all those things, but I was earning money in order to work instead. I was earning work time, to overcome the most common barrier for a beginning writer and, indeed, throughout one's whole life.

After the war, a new avenue opened to writers besides newspaper work and, for a few, Hollywood. Academia presented the opportunity for writers to teach what one of the best, at Duke, insisted on calling "Composition." I have seen so many writers make this choice, only to be caught in the tangle of their earning, so that gradually what I call *work* has become an avocation, and their energies are spent in a way they never intended. But it happens so gradually, and it is so dangerous, that many an unhappy English professor has wasted sweetness, not on desert air but on the job that is most seductive of all, the care of the young, most of whom have no idea of the daily, monthly, yearly drain of sacrifice.

Then, in 1946, I used what I had learned; after all, I had had postgraduate training in journalism from some of the best. I set out to be a freelance journalist as far as the world of publishing was concerned. And I rationed my time, and my energy, so that what for me was the only work worth doing came first. I set aside the time to make a living.

Then there was, and still is, *the suit*. It became a joke in my family and among my friends. The suit was still the same one I had worn on my day of deliverance in New York, and in the limousine on the way to the fine wedding. Now it was kept for magazine editors, for publishing, for wherever I could present myself to make suggestions that would give me the month's survival income. It was my uniform, and I saw to it that it never showed blood, never showed poverty, never showed lack of respect for what I had chosen to do to earn the fuel for my work.

Through those years, as far as the outside world was concerned, I was, I hope, a good and dependable freelance journalist. I wrote about fashion; I wrote about textiles; I wrote speeches; and for a while I actually wrote about manners as Mrs. Charles Palmer, etiquette expert for the English magazine *Woman's Own*.

My biography in the magazine noted that I lived in a "well-appointed" house in Wiltshire, had a daughter who, if I remember correctly, was a debutante. My picture in *Woman's Own* showed a lady with a dark sweater and pearls, her hair swept up. Oh, what dignity was there! I was dressed for the photograph in the editor's clothes.

Four people lived on the twenty pounds a month I picked up for that job—myself, Den (who by then had moved to Cornwall), Christopher, and a poet who will still be nameless, who was working on a long poem and received ten bob a week from an anonymous admirer. I was at that point living in the tithe barn of the vicarage in Mevagissy in Cornwall. I made my own shirts, wore jeans, the inevitable duffle coat, sneakers, cut my own hair, and during those apprentice years wrote six plays, all of which were praised but none produced, yet there were some fine dinners and lunches in the theater district.

I had taken Christopher to Cornwall while I was convalescing, first to Zennor, where D. H. Lawrence had retreated with Frieda after she had run away with him from a house in Well Walk—which had a plaque that said that it had been Constable's house. We found out together—he seven, I a grown-up—that Zennor was appallingly and frighteningly haunted. It was a mist that swirled around us both, so bad that on the second day we agreed to leave the farmhouse where we had taken a room and walk back to St. Ives.

There we were, both of us in Wellington boots, slogging down a wet road in Cornwall, stopping at round stones, cromlechs, and ruins all along the way. It was the beginning of years in Cornwall, off and on—partly because of my health and partly because the apartment in Camden Town had been ruined by the opening in the mews, just under our windows, of a black-market garage where stolen cars were brought in for their license plates to be changed. It was a very noisy, banging-on-metal, swearing, police-raid-prone, and general postwar, wild-boy meeting place.

For a while, we were schooling Christopher at home, first in the barn and then, for the winter, as caretakers in a beautiful house set on a bluff above the English Channel where Tristan was supposed to have jumped into a waiting boat to escape King Marke after delivering a much-used Isolde.

11

MR. ELIOT

◦⁓◦

There are days, usually events, that photograph themselves so in your memory that you carry their details. Some are national—the day Roosevelt died, the day Kennedy was shot. This day was personal, and secret. It was 1946, in London, and I was going to meet Mr. Eliot. I had dressed very carefully, in my suit and the last nylons I had brought from New York. I carried a telegram in my pocket. It was an invitation from Morley Kennerly, one of the editors at Faber and Faber. We had no telephone. Phones were hard to come by that year in London—phones and food and enough sleep and sweets and nylons and enough money to live. Austerity was the catchword for those years after the war. It was dry and tired and quiet. Its color was gray.

But that day, I remember, was clear and sunny, so rare in England. Dry leaves skittered across the Albert Road under the front wheels of the number 74 bus. I sat on the top deck in the front seat, not apprehensive but frozen in expectation. Why are we so drawn to meeting those who have already given us more than we have asked? What did I expect of Eliot? What is it that makes us think that some magic will rub off? If only? What? Dreams as banal as dreams of movie stars and royalty? Are they dreams of notice? Reassurance? That the written

word that has become a treasured part of your own memory
will turn human?

It was, and is, a hard world for writers. However we see ourselves or kick against the pricks, we are piece workers in a cot-
tage industry that today has made itself into a big-board
monster. We forget what it was like to make the choice to be a
writer, earn a living to pay for the choice, to work with only the
hope of being published someday. In my case, it would be eight
more years of catch-as-catch-can freelance journalism before I
sold a novel. I remember now that the hope was for his recognition, not of anything as obvious as talent or fame, more a
hope for recognition of a peerage of intent—some sense of the
familiar, as if we had already known each other. It was that he
might know what I was trying to do, more than I knew myself,
hope for an ease, for permission at last to speak.

We all shared a neural awareness that year. It came from a
deep relief that we mistook for energy. Noises were louder, as
they are when you are sleepless on cold nights alone. I remember a woman standing in a queue at a bus stop, letting the tears
run down her almost-expressionless face.

Relief and fatigue together made us more aware of each
other than we would ever be again, overconscious of work not
yet done, of sensuous essences, of all we had ignored. The city
was dusty. The ruins and neglected gardens were wild with
weeds that year, and on Primrose Hill the cabbages were shaggy
in the allotments. I had squandered four years of war—four
years of repressing what talent I might have been developing.
My English friends had lost six. We were starting late. We knew
it. We talked and talked. We longed for assurance. Even before
the war ended, T. S. Eliot had given it to us.

When the war had gone on too long, and the right and
wrong of its beginning had drifted into terrible pragmatic deci-

sions to get it over with at any cost; when the voices we had trusted sounded shrill and we knew we had been fooled but didn't know quite how and were too old for our years; when hope seemed a luxury, slogans naive, and what writing existed was propaganda, Eliot's poem "Little Gidding" had been published in England.[1]

Here was the voice of "The Waste Land," which between the wars had made despair a fashion. Almost alone, he had gone on writing. He had somehow refined what he had to tell us, beyond the banality of disappointment and hopelessness, into a promise of steel. The accepted premise is that little poetry truly reflects World War II. But there is "Little Gidding." When I go back to it, as to a place that is a poem, it shakes me with recall.

In 1946, among the ruins I passed on the 74 bus route, the "dust in the air" still existed. The exposed walls where there had been homes were cleaned, neglected, empty husks snaggled like missing teeth along the rows of houses. The intimacy of wallpaper was stained by rain. We took that cityscape for granted, as we took the rationing, the queues, the slow tenderness of recovery. In 1946, there had been too many deaths of men of our fathers' generation who were victims of wartime fatigue.

Too many of us had involved ourselves in "things ill-done and done to others' harm / Which once you took for exercise of virtue." Eliot was of that generation, yet he had defined for us the mistakes, the years of "wrong to wrong," and had recognized the true courage that was not rhetorical. He had led us through our necessary recognitions as through a minefield, had stripped us of whatever communal illusions were left over

---

[1] "Little Gidding" was published in 1942, the fourth poem in *The Four Quartets*, which was published in England in 1944.—AHF.

from a more innocent time. Then he had the miraculous effrontery of spirit to promise that "all shall be well."

Even now, when I say, "we" and "us," I sense a need that was so strong then, to define those words lest we be fooled again by communal illusions. They did not mean the voice of "a generation"—we no longer allowed ourselves that faceless deception—but "we," you and me, in this room or another room, a real "we" who spoke a common language and, in Eliot's words, were trying not to "cease from exploration."

He had also told us, in words as clear as Hamlet's advice to the players, and much like it, how to write: "The common word exact without vulgarity, / The formal word precise but not pedantic, /The complete consort dancing together."

He became our father to revere and kick against. We wrote for him our private work that he would never see. We exchanged glimpses of him. Someone had seen Mr. Eliot and Djuna Barnes dancing solemnly together through Soho Square at midnight. Someone else had seen him standing in a queue for a visa at the American Embassy, when most people of his fame and stature would have expected privilege. There are a thousand Londons, each a small city; and in the city of literary fame, no one really hides there.

This was the man I was actually going to meet. I had already been there a hundred times, in the same room. Expected rooms are large. The light would be bright, the air full of wit and the musical clink of glasses in some bright Literary London that never was nor ever will be. There would be twenty people there, and they would all be famous and familiar with one another. A few of us, the unpublished young, would sit below the salt and catch, from time to time, revealing nuances, memorable words, needed advice thrown like scraps at a banquet.

Sunlight was our luxury that year, almost the only one. I remember especially the colors in the sun that day. I changed buses. I prayed not to be late. I looked down from the top deck on soldiers from one of the Guards regiments as they marched toward the palace in their new uniforms, an astonishing red after the years of dust-colored battle dress. I remember that and the yellow of the leaves and on a few doorways new primary colors made brighter that day by the sun.

I have forgotten the address. I only remember that my heart sank when I walked toward the house. I was in a crescent, I think, or a square. I shuffled dry leaves in front of my unaccustomed high-heeled shoes. I walked more and more slowly, and I was afraid. It was one of those charming cul-de-sacs of pretty little townhouses. Not one of them could have had a room where twenty people could be given lunch. I rang the doorbell. A maid answered and led me up a flight of narrow stairs in an attractive hall to one of those second-floor drawing rooms in small London houses. There was no sound of people. Silence, Sunday silence. Behind a closed door at the front of the house I heard a far-too-quiet murmur of voices. The maid opened the door for me.

Not war, not bombs, not riding motorcycles behind dispatch riders, not low-flying when I was in the Women's Auxiliary Air Force of the RAF, none of it produces in me the memory of heart-shaking panic I had when I stepped inside that room and the door shut behind me and I saw them.

Three men. My host, Morley Kennerly, near the door, was mixing martinis. Beside the fireplace sat a man in a wheelchair who had the reputation of being the most vituperative literary critic in London. It was John Hayward. I knew that Mr. Eliot shared a flat with him. Cynics said that he was Eliot's cross to bear. Shadowed against the sunny window was Mr. Eliot. I saw only a dark shape.

I suppose we were introduced. I know that my host handed me a martini. My hand shook so that the drink began to spill over my fingers. Someone took the glass from me, took my wet hand in his, led me across the small room, sat me down on a sofa beside him, handed me his handkerchief and then the drink again, and began to ask, not talk, about the day.

It was Mr. Eliot. Within minutes, I was sipping the drink, telling about the soldiers in their new red uniforms, at ease, in all the term's military sense, for I had learned too well the fear-of-father discipline of the armed forces.

But he was not to know that. He didn't know me. He only knew that someone was terrified, and he comforted, instinctively, without a question or a hint of condescension. Perhaps the things we learn most deeply we learn in timeless moments. I remember thinking, "How can he bear the compassion he suffers?" The man was purely humble, purely kind; he had a gentle, genial face. No wonder that, like a hermit crab, he had to be protected by the borrowed shell of stricter habits, ecclesiastical disciplines, asceticism, and, above all, friends.

John Hayward seemed to take a cue from him. Even he was charming, entertaining, anecdotal, though, alas for the literary "tat" collectors, I have forgotten most of the stories. It was only a pleasant, easy lunch—four people sitting at a table in a small house in Chelsea, forgettable to three of them, I am sure, but not to me. Never in the three hours we sat there did he leave me out. He leaned across the table once and said, "We know that, but . . ." What I had said, I don't know. It is the "we" I remember.

He was playful. He told about trying to learn the ukulele by correspondence, "to impress the girls." He practiced with a flashlight, tented under the covers in a London boardinghouse so his landlady wouldn't hear him. I see now that he was being a little flirtatious. I would not have dared to recognize it then.

He said he took Thursday off from the office. I asked him if he did his own work then. He laughed and said, "Oh, no. I write the blurbs for Faber and Faber books. It's easier to do it at home."

He told me about rejections. He said he kept a scrapbook of rejected letters to *The Times of London*, the letters column that was the most important barometer of opinion in England for years.

He was, to me, American. He had not lost an easygoing, Middle Western pleasantness. I saw nothing—nothing at all—of the imitation Englishman that people said he had become, even though by then London had been his home for more than thirty years. His voice, like mine, was still American, but he had lost much of his accent. This happens anyplace, especially if one has a sensitive ear. French improves in Paris, German in Vienna. So in London, after a long time, we both spoke English with British precision and our own vowel sounds. In the late afternoon, we strolled along Cheyne Walk together as he pushed John Hayward's wheelchair. There are memories of other times—tea at Cheyne Walk in a half-empty flat, his small office at Faber and Faber. He stands like my father, his hands against his back, his arms akimbo, and he is grinning at something. I lived most of the time outside of London later. The friendship had hardly existed, and then it faded to nothing.

But more than the other images, it is necessary to remember the first day I met him, to call back that rare kindness and compassion, to set that portrait up against the others. The domain of his fame has made T. S. Eliot public beyond the knowledge of his friends. Both Peter Ackroyd's biography, which is benign but depends on the legend, and the play *Tom and Viv*, which is based in part on malicious gossip, present a glimpsed and fugitive public figure. None of us can set the record straight. We see from where we stand and remember what we knew. I can only recall the man and his work as I saw them, when they were new to me. I want to honor a debt he would never have dreamed I owed him.

12

CORONATION[1]

∽

I t was the first of June, 1953, and the night was old and smelled of rain. That night is so strong in my memory that I can go there anytime. To keep from losing it, I tried to write about it as soon as I got home, before I slept. I put it in among those papers that grow like fungus, on their own, and then, sometime in all the moves, house to house, country to country, they were thrown away.

I find that I don't need the notes. Nothing is lost. I relive it, the night, the color, all of it, for it was the night that, for a million people, the war was finally over, the grayness, the rationing, the dimming of spirit that had been daily life since 1945.

England shook itself awake. Voices were raised, little knots of people who had claimed their places on the coronation route were singing; the air was full of mist and people and a kind of mob joy.

About eleven o'clock the night before the coronation, six of

[1] Judging from the evidence in Mary Lee's computer files, she began to write this piece in Kinsale, Virginia, on July 22, 2004, and expanded it in Ivy on October 11, 2004, while she was recovering from pneumonia and devoting most of her attention to the first draft of *Tom*.—AHF.

us went together on the crowded tube to Trafalgar Square. One of the party was the kind of person who had memorized the coronation route.[2] I thought it was her own pickiness, which I found annoying. I like mistakes. But it wasn't. She was English, Putney English, and like a million other people of London, she had studied one of the maps printed in the papers to make certain that we would find a place to wait.

The statue in the center of Trafalgar Square was already covered with clinging boys and girls, who had found a perfect place above the crowd. Below them, a London bobby was trying to persuade them to come down. He would have had as much luck with the boys and girls as he would with the statue of Lord Nelson trying to get them to walk off the plinth they occupied as victors.

From the square, through Pall Mall, groups of people had taken possession of their bit of the pavement. Men going into their clubs apologized for disturbing them. There had been an estimate of a million people, but it seemed like a series of small family or friendly groups instead. It was intimate.

We strolled along the route from Trafalgar Square, up Piccadilly, over to Pall Mall, as near as we could get to Westminster Abbey. All the way, as we crossed and recrossed the route, there were small sidewalk statements of ownership. Nobody stood; we found out why later.

Calls back and forth, a little rain, there was warmth among them all; we had not yet reached that state. The hint of rain was cold; we saw them as huddling against it.

Finally, up the Mall, which was solid with people, we turned into Hyde Park beyond the arch with Boadicea on her

[2] It was a circuitous, seven-mile route from Buckingham Palace to Westminster Abbey, where Elizabeth II was to be crowned by the Archbishop of Canterbury on June 2.—AHF.

war chariot with knives set along the wheels. At last, there was room for us. We took possession of a little place and stood there wondering if we would be able to see when the coronation procession would pass fifteen hours later.

It was then that we realized why everyone was sitting down. A small woman sitting on a pillow just at the edge of the street pulled at my duffle coat. "Sit down now," she told us. We were surprised enough to obey her. Then, when we had marked our places, she added, "so you won't have to stand later." We gathered around her. We had, like thousands of others, made a group, and she instructed us on how one can look at a queen.

13

NINE YEARS

❦

I had been working for nine years; I had finally turned the last play into a so-called novel—to me it was still a play. But if the years of work only produced many delightful friends, good dinners, and all the gossip and disappointment that I had once yearned for, it was time to stop.

So I decided to write a play in the form of a novel. I would be all the actors, the set designer, the props, the director. So, armed with this self-imposed dictatorship of the material, I hid out in the tithe barn in Mevagissey and wrote a novel called *Deed*. It went to every American publisher my agent in New York could think of, and every publisher in London that I could think of. I had a one hundred percent pure and perfect international refusal.

In the meantime, I took a walk with my friend James Broughton in the neglected, weed-covered gardens where what had survived time and war from the 1851 Great Exhibition in London had been moved. It was surreal. Dinosaurs, woolly mammoths, great Galapagos tortoises sat among the weeds and small trees. James was looking at it for a set for his documentary, which was called *The Pleasure Garden* when it was produced in 1953.

We argued on high matters of art and life. It had been a long lunch. The argument had reached an impasse when he said that art reflected life, and I said, no, it defines undefined life, and the way it is perceived is as important as the original work. Tragedy must be perceived as tragedy.

I said, why if the tragedy of *Phedre* were to happen in a small American city, Phedre would be perceived as either mutton dressed as lamb, a victim of her own menopause, a joke, or a subject of short-lived gossip. James, of course, disagreed. So I said, "All right. I will show you."

So I set out to write *Phedre*. It had no title yet. I made a workroom in the house in Well Walk; I hung a calendar and an outline on the wall and stayed there day and night until I had a first draft on paper. The finished book went to every American publisher. It was rejected.

14

MAUGHAM[1]

❧

Like Semele who longed to see God and was wrapped in
fire which consumed her, so I longed for fame and was
destroyed by it.

Peter Ackroyd, *The Last Testament of Oscar Wilde*

My book *The Love Eaters* was accepted by Heinemann in
London on October 30, 1953. I know because the date is
in a letter from Somerset Maugham, inviting me to lunch in
his suite at the Dorchester Hotel in London at one o'clock. I
still have the letter, and every two or three years I look at it
again to bring back the day, like taking a pill for something
that has long gone—just in case.

He asked me to bring Angus Wilson, England's most pres-
tigious and fashionable writer at the time. I admired Wilson
and still do. He was a mentor to me. His rare combination of

---

[1] Mary Lee wrote this essay in 1987 in response to an unfavorable review of her
novel *Celebration*. In the last paragraph of the essay, she provides the chronology
by saying she is "sixty-eight" and that "thirty-four years" have passed. This indi-
cates that she had not yet worked this essay into the time frame for *Learning to
Fly*.—AHF.

social awareness and style was a goal I only hoped for. In 1953, I saw him every day at the beginning of his critical success—praise beyond my own wildest dreams. I was a young writer whose fiction had not yet been published and who, having made a vow not to take a "regular" job until I had bought myself time to write, made a precarious living writing fashion and "cultural" journalism. At that point, Maugham, in his eightieth year, was as heavy with honors and fortune as any writer in the world.

I remember thinking, when I read the Heinemann letter, how auspicious it was, after ten years of apprenticeship, to celebrate with those two, the newest and the most established, that day of all days. It seemed to be magic, a dream membership in a faraway circle of acceptance and understanding. I took some pride in going, as usual, to the British Museum to work on my current book, *O Beulah Land*. I told myself that I had not let ten years of rejection stop me, and I certainly was not going to let acceptance do it. I think I saw acceptance then as some great gold curtain parting, like the beginning announcement of the Saturday afternoon opera broadcasts from the old Met, which I had listened to when I was growing up.

I had first met Somerset Maugham in early October; I had gone in fear and trembling to interview him at the Dorchester with two layouts for *Look* magazine with photographs taken when he was making a speech in America. The article was to celebrate his eightieth birthday. My assignment was to ask him for remarks that would serve as captions.

I wore, I remember, low-heeled shoes. He was a short man, and I had been warned that he was oversensitive, sarcastic, unkind. He looked the part—the creased, bitter saurian face, the downturned mouth of Graham Sutherland's portrait and the cold photograph by Yousuf Karsh. I had studied them both

and whatever else I could find, and I looked forward to the
afternoon with a mixture of excitement and dread. I had been
told that he had an appalling stammer, which terrified me
because I, too, stammer when I am tired or when I am with
another stammerer. I had a sick vision of us gobbling and gasp-
ing at each other. I stood in the lobby of the Dorchester and my
voice shook when I asked to be announced.

Mr. Maugham's secretary, Alan Searle, answered the door
and told me that he was still taking his nap. He apologized and
left me to wait and tremble. I can still see the room, the two soft
sofas set on either side of a dead fireplace in a parody of a
country-house living room, the muted colors of expensive
cloth, the heavy silk curtains, the reproductions of antiques,
the soundless carpet. I began to relax. Nothing makes me feel
more secure than the rich anonymity of a luxury hotel room. I
was at that point living in a communal house with bare floors
in Chelsea where color covered poverty and visual wit, empti-
ness. I found such dumb pastel luxury, even through the nerv-
ousness, a comfort.

Mr. Maugham came and stood for a second in the doorway.
He was small, shy, and plump. He was dressed in old tweeds
with patches at the elbows. The downturned lines by his mouth
were gone. He was smiling. He called me "my dear," and not
once in the three hours that followed did he stammer.

Now I must find his voice, or his voice for that day, and this
is the way I remember it. "I know why you are here," he said, as
if we had met in Aladdin's cave, which, for me, we had, there on
that cozy, warm, late afternoon with the early evening lowering
outside. "Now, let me see the layouts. We can get these out of
the way." He sat down on one of the sofas with the layouts on
a coffee table in front of him. There were two full pages, and he
went through them as if he were reading captions already

there. "Let's see now. What on earth would I have been saying when I looked like that? Something about America, I think. They [the mysterious "they"] always like for me to say something about America. You Americans (that single English word for us) are so self-conscious, my dear."

So he went through picture after picture. "Something about France. They always like something about France . . . and sex . . . and changes in the world. . . ." When he had finished, he handed the layouts to me and lounged back on the sofa. I could hear the tea cart rumbling along the hall outside the room. The whole process, including the arrival of tea, had taken less than half an hour. When that cozy rite was finished and the waiter had left, he said with a sigh, as if he had been doing the washing, "Now, that's done, my dear. We can talk. Tell me about yourself."

What could I tell him? That I had worked for fashion magazines? That I had been in the war? That I was working every day in the Reading Room of the British Museum on a novel that I had no hope for, since novels about history were denigrated as unfashionable? My other two unpublished novels? My six unproduced plays? No, nothing to tell. He didn't wait for me to tell him nothing.

"I love my yearly visit to London," he said for a beginning, and then he went on for most of the afternoon, as the night came down outside. He was anecdotal, entertaining, warm, and, dare I say, sweet, but he really was, the man with the reputation of a snapping turtle. I was embarrassed at staying so long, but he charmed me into it. I realize as I write, so many years later, that Alan Searle had gone out and that Mr. Maugham did not want to be left alone. He was old. He had a new and very willing ear, unjudging and young. I was babysitting for Searle.

I forgot that it was an "interview" and simply asked questions gleaned from the homework I had done. I wanted to know why, with all the successful plays he had written, he had let someone else write the most memorable, *Rain*. He was a conjurer. We were not in London in the dim afternoon. We were in Hollywood in 1920, white Spanish houses, sand, palms, sunshine, Keystone Cops, and Pearl White. He sat one evening, he said, on the patio of The Garden of Allah, the legendary cluster of cottages where visiting screenwriters stayed in the early days of silent Hollywood. Then he continued:

John Colton was a friend of mine who was staying there, too. He came out and sat down beside me, and told me that he had not slept for several nights. He looked terrible, dark circles and all. I had the proofs of a book of short stories that had just come in the mail for me. I threw it to him, and said, "Here, these will put you to sleep."

The next morning he came out on the patio again. He looked worse. "Dammit, Willy, I haven't slept a wink," he told me. "Why haven't you made a play of that story *Sadie Thompson*?" Now, you must understand that I of all people knew what a play was. After all, I had three hit plays running in London at the same time. I told him so. He asked me if he could try. I said, "Of course, but you're wasting your time."

When the play he called *Rain* opened in Boston, you could have bought it for five thousand dollars. It ran for six years and killed the loveliest actress I have ever known, Jeanne Eagels. I saw her one evening do a glorious performance, and when she came off stage, she fainted. She had been playing with a safety pin stabbing her in the side, and when we undressed her, the blood had nearly soaked through her clothes.

Sometimes he didn't wait for me to ask a question. "I know what you're going to ask. I know you're here because I'm going to be eighty soon. Changes in the world, they always ask about changes in the world." He jumped up. "Now I know you expect me to talk about wars, and all that. But you forget that I was trained as a doctor. No. Not war. 'The modern contraceptive.' That's what has changed the world. In the old days," he said, as he began to play an imaginary game of tennis around the room, "we lobbed the ball gently over the net so the lady we were playing with could hobble over gracefully and lob it back. Now!" His face changed. He crouched down. "We stand at back center court and fight for our lives!"

I asked him what it felt like to publish his first book in 1897, the same year the greats like Henry James, Joseph Conrad, H. G. Wells, and Rudyard Kipling were bringing out some of their most famous novels.

"Oh, were they?" he said vaguely. "My dear, we weren't paying any attention to 'them.' We were reading George Meredith. He was our god. We all learned from him. Nobody reads Meredith now. You can tell from the bad prose. Conrad? James? Oh come, come, who were they? It was Meredith. Have you read him?" I was afraid to say no. "I can see you haven't. Read him. You read Meredith."

He said, "You know, one of my pleasures when I come on my visit to London is to meet some of the new writers. Now, there is a young man called Angus Wilson. I would love to meet him. Do you know him?"

I was able to tell him with some pride that I saw Angus Wilson every day. He was still working in the Reading Room, and writing at night and on weekends. I knew he was working on a novel. I was even so bemused by the afternoon's warmth that I thought it possible to suggest that I give them both dinner.

"My dear, that is kind. But you see, I don't really like to go out at night, and I think it best if you brought Mr. Wilson here for luncheon. Now where would I write to invite him?"

I'm afraid that the next morning at the Reading Room, I gushed to Angus. I said, "Everybody is wrong about Mr. Maugham. He's as benign as Santa Claus. He wants to meet you. I told him you were working very hard on a book, but that you might."

"I wouldn't miss it for the world," Angus said, with less ecstasy and more irony.

Even in the taxi to the Dorchester that day, I babbled on about the magic coincidence of my book being accepted on such a day, and about what a surprise Mr. Maugham was going to be to him. There were no more fears when I called Alan Searle and told him we were there.

Maugham stood a few feet behind Searle, framed by the room. He was his portrait and his reputation. He wore another face—reptilian, defensive, cold. His clothes were *de rigueur* for bankers in the city—the black jacket, the pin-striped trousers, the dead-white collar, the black tie, daring faint stripes. Outside of shaking hands, he never spoke to me but twice in the next two terrible hours. I had brought Angus Wilson into a literary lion's den. I was a Chinese go-between, nothing else. We all sat down on the two sofas. Searle poured martinis from a pitcher.

I realized, of course, what had happened. Angus Wilson was a rival and a threat. I had not been. I had been an interlude, probably forgotten. Wilson was, for that day, all the enemies that paranoid man had had to contend with for his later writing life. Unfair? Of course it was unfair. Wilson was and is the most generous critic and writer in England, more helpful to the young than Maugham ever thought of being, a fine stylist, a natural teacher. Like every good teacher, I can still hear his voice as, in casual conversation at the Reading Room, he would give me clue after clue, generous and subtle and right. One, that genius can only be imitated, not learned from—"Study Stacy Aumonier to learn to construct a short story," I hear him say. "Craft. That's what we can learn from other writers, not genius."

But that day, as a new contender in that arena I did not yet know, he had to fight. I hardly remember Maugham taking his eyes off Angus. Question after question. There was not a leading writer who had visited his house on Cap Ferrat that Maugham did not destroy. My idols and mentors fell, one after another. He accused this one of drunkenness, that one of dirty habits, T. S. Eliot of stealing his books. Alan Searle and I just looked at each other and drank martinis.

At last I heard the lunch trolley being wheeled down the hall, and the waiter came in and set up a table in the room.

Maugham sat at its head, Searle at the foot; Angus and I sat at either side. By the time lunch came, Maugham was stammering so badly that I could see that part of the arrogant head-thrown-back look was his habitual attempt to recover his voice. He had one of the worst stammers I have ever heard, and, needless to say, I wouldn't have dared open my mouth had he given me a chance to.

Finally, though, he looked at me, from high above my face. "We're having p-p-p-p-partridge for lunch," he said. "Would you like i-i-i-ice cream or ch-ch-cheese to follow?"

Very, very carefully, I said, "Cheese."

He put his nose very close to Angus's face and, a little ominously, asked, "Ch-ch-cheese or i-i-i-ice-cream?"

Angus said, "Cheese."

"You know"—the voice was gossipy, not imperious for a minute—"F-f-f-f-frank S-s-s-s-swinnerton was here the other day. He said ice cream!"

Angus said, "Really? I shouldn't have thought he was that sort of man."

It was like that all through lunch, every remark weighed and weighed again, all the signs secret among the English, the Literati, and the Accepted were brought out, tested, some found wanting, some passed, as the cheese.

At one point, having bullied the absent, there was a shift. It was time, almost formally, to bully Alan Searle.

"My dear," Maugham said, but the phrase was no longer kind, "Alan here knows *everybody* worth knowing. Alan knew Festing Jones!"

I didn't realize that this was supposed to be a joke. I had just been reading Samuel Butler, and Festing Jones was his close friend. I was delighted to be able to talk to Searle. "Did you really?" I said. "Was it true that Butler asked him and another friend to spread his ashes over Lincoln's Inn Fields as a final joke? I see two old men in their top hats, dancing around, strewing ashes."

Maugham was furious, like a child. He commanded a dead silence at the table. Angus Wilson came to the rescue, as he would. "Mary Lee has just had her first book accepted this morning."

"Oh, really," voice of ice. "What publisher?"

"Yours." I got my small revenge, fifty years younger than he was, full of martinis, and robbed of Festing Jones.

Hyde Park is just across Park Lane from the Dorchester. I didn't leave. I escaped. All the rest of the daylight I wandered in the park. It was damp, and a mist was in the distance. It smelled of autumn, which is different from our fall, a lying down, no dry wind, no deep frost, damp and dying. I thought of what I had seen and heard of fame, and of that man, who had had so many honors, so much money, and all the public praise that a long career could give him, and who still stammered like a neglected small boy when he was faced with any competition. I saw the face, not as vicious but as etched with years of pain and bitterness.

"If that is fame, I don't ever want it," I told the trees, and the martinis and the afternoon.

I knew I couldn't help being an alchemist, transmuting the raw material of life into fiction. It was and is for me a function as obsessive as an oyster making a pearl, an activity that can only be understood by experiencing it, not to be analyzed by outside observers. But there were things I could help. I could help letting reputation shadow my soul, as Maugham had done, and at the same time, I remembered the kind, gentle man hidden within him that I had seen a few weeks earlier. I could help being etched as he was by acceptance or denial. I saw that it was not fame itself but the seeking of fame that could destroy.

I even considered not publishing at all if that was its end. But I rejected that. Not even the martinis or the experience or the cold that was creeping over the park and making me shiver could make that seem anything but self-defeating. We do, as Emily Dickinson said, write our letters to the world, and we want the world to read them.

I had a son to raise, and I needed what money I could glean from the small advances I was condemned to for so long. All this in an afternoon in the park, drunken resolution and paraphrase, swearing on the altar of God, eternal vigilance against any form of literary tyranny over my mind.

I vowed to find my energy from within and not from reputation and to avoid the "literary" life. I resolved to be grateful for understanding and praise and honors if they came, but never to hang on them, and after what books I would write—how many then I had no idea of—to forget publishing as soon as I could and get back to work.

Now, more than thirty years later, and to my shame, a single adverse and smart-aleck review of my book *Celebration* by a "remote and ineffectual don" at Oxford, has triggered this recall to warn me once again that I, too, can fall victim to that most familiar of industrial hazards as a writer—literary paranoia. Never mind that the other reviews have been more than favorable, this one thorn sticks, and I must face some regrettable facts before I can pull it out.

Since that fall day in London in 1953, I have faced the public a dozen times with a book in my hand, like Rousseau, as a gift that I see being thrown over the heads of the reviewers to the people who want to read it, like contraceptives in Dublin Airport. Financially, I must stand or fall in the literary industry of New York, as specialized and distilled a center as that of the diamond and gold merchants who flock together on Forty-seventh Street.

Have I kept the resolutions I made that day? Like New Year's resolutions—only haltingly. Neither the experience I had then, nor any since, has fully armed me for the diminishing act of having to make public a book on which I have spent several private years. Nothing in my necessarily isolated way of living prepares me for the sea change that goes on for a few months—of becoming public, a target and an object, alas, whether I am praised or blamed. The very qualities that make me and most writers what we are also ill-suit us for what we have to do.

What I did not know then was that it is the exposure that palls; intelligent praise mitigates it, a godsend, a palliative. We must go through publishing, alas, when we are most vulnerable, bankrupt with fatigue, when we have spent energy deep into our *élan vital* to finish books. Fortunately, it only happens once every two or three years. I don't think most of us could stand it oftener. It is more primitive and more frightening than facing the reviewers. But anxiety and fatigue can charge reviewing with more importance than it ought to possess.

I cannot deny that I have gone through all the crises of having to publish, and I have been hurt, though never stopped by them. I have had to remind myself over and over that the impetus is outside and predictable: a few real lovers of good writing who read before they judge, a few fine writers who are occasional critics, good luck or bad luck, bad editorial choice of reviewers, professional reviewers with graduate-student mentalities, who make their livings "approving of what is approved of" or grinding abstract axes in public. I have felt their tiny pitons as they have climbed my back toward their careers. When this happens to me, I am tempted by the dying words of Auguste Comte, "Only one man ever understood me, and he didn't understand me."

I have hated as much as anyone else being a victim of careless reviewers from the burgeoning academic industry. They remind me of the portrait in *Huckleberry Finn* of the girl who "had two arms folded across her breast, and two arms stretched out in front, and two more reaching up toward the moon." One academic eye is on the book as raw material for acceptable theory. When I am charged with those twin illusions of MFA programs, point of view and characterization, I feel as though I have submitted my book to a "creative writing" workshop in hell.

Then there is another eye on this year's critical fashion, another eye on The Department, and yet another eye on the Sunday book sections or weeklies I call "The Literary Reviews of Tenure." Alas, having regular jobs and having to publish or perish, they work cheaply, and budget-obsessed editors do no honor to writing by overhiring them. By the rules of politeness in publishing, we novelists are supposed to allow ourselves to be used as fuel for job-holding—derided, misunderstood, and compared to death without a word of protest.

No writer I know who has achieved a reputation after years of work has escaped having it thrown back in his or her face. I am reminded of the young, poor poets trashing T. S. Eliot in London pubs in the early fifties, or young would-be novelists decrying the reputations of Graham Greene, Henry Green, Somerset Maugham, and Angus Wilson, or any other famous writer who had succeeded after long years in that most unforgivable of activities—earning money and critical acceptance.

Alas, I too have been "listed"—that lazy, critical habit of making categories instead of reading. There are lists of Southern writers, Jewish writers, Suburban writers, Post-Modernists, Minimalists, Maximalists, Premenstrualists, the Sensitive, the Important, and what a friend calls the I'm So Fucking Lonely School of American Writing. Finally, there is the list of THE GREAT, those who have outlasted their contemporaries, where it helps to be unread, old, male, grouchy, foreign, Eudora Welty, or dead. Finally, I say, like the boy in *Zéro de Conduite*, "Monsieur le Professor, je vous dis merde."

In those few months of public life, we tend to protect ourselves with false nostalgia. Once there were better reviewers.

Once there was grace and honor in publishing. This is nonsense. There never was. The marketplace does not change, and Herman Melville still stands awkwardly at literary teas, ignored by Margaret Fuller.

All we ever have had to defend us is time. Time will give to the destructive, ambitious critic a footnote as it did to Lockhart, the once-feared editor of the *Edinburgh Review*. Now he is mentioned, if at all, because of his advice given to the little chemist (Keats) to go back to his pots, and his devastating review of *Wuthering Heights*. He has become a bad joke, a parody, a reductio ad absurdum of all critics.

Melville died forgotten. Conrad's honors came too late. Faulkner had already been too wounded when long-earned recognition came. When Scott Fitzgerald died, just forty-four years old, people thought he had been dead for years. Poor Stendhal and Melville dead provide livings to academics who act as hatchet men on the living. Few of those we revere now escaped the exhaustion of neglect and denial. I will not be fooled like this. Kemal Atatürk once said that there was no such thing as a victim; there were only people who allowed themselves to be victimized.

So, at the age of sixty-eight, I have made myself encounter not only Somerset Maugham and Angus Wilson that day in London thirty-four years ago but also the young writer that I was then, so sure that I would not fall victim to my own weaknesses. The recall of those resolves sustains me, though, and replaces despond with anger, if not forgiveness. Better to be sustained by arrogance and curse the night than descend to mournful self-defense, or the bitterness that etched the face of Somerset Maugham.

15

MY PARIS

～

In the fall of 1949, Den and I went, for the first time to France. We chose the New Haven to Dieppe Channel crossing because, although it was the longest, it was also the cheapest. Five hours on the Channel in late fall was all that bad-tempered stretch of sea was said to be. The wind did not that day sit fair for France.

We dodged between half-submerged wrecks that had not yet been moved since the Dieppe commando raids that had failed and the D-Day air raids that had succeeded. The Dieppe commando raid had been a disaster; too many people knew about it and too many people talked. The Germans had been waiting for the Canadian commandos. Most of them were killed, some were imprisoned.

We stood on deck and looked down at what was left of the war. Some of the hulls were marked by rusty iron prows thrust above the water's surface; some were underwater shadows, with only a radio antenna a few inches above the water to mark its grave.

First, for us, France was a scent, the scent of food and wine. And sun, blessed sun on the dirty dock. We found places on the train to Gare St. Lazare, the last stop on the poverty path to

Paris. The food on the train unrationed and good, the easy glass of wine after the wild sea when we dared not let go of glasses; France already seemed to us, compared to England, a luxury.

On the train to Paris, in Gare St. Lazare, along the streets of Paris, we smelled an exotic mixture of wine and food and salad dressing. That, for us, was the first sense of Paris. When a salad or a soup has that scent, I know I have succeeded as a cook. We had come from the years of stark rationing in London. It had a name: Austerity. We did a lot of thinking about food.

Paris was still dirty and war-worn. On so many street corners, especially in the Sixth Arrondissement, there were small shrines to the people in the FFI, the Free French Resistance. Albert Camus had been a member in Paris. A dear friend I knew later, who taught with me at Bard College, had been a fifteen-year-old Jewish boy disguised as a delivery boy, carrying messages from cell to cell as he bicycled across Paris during the occupation. When he, as a middle-aged man, received the Croix de Guerre, most of the students did not know what it was, nor did they bother to find out.

Most of the remembered dead were teenagers, who had been shot by retreating Germans during the liberation of Paris. China plaques with their names and their ages, with little vases of fresh flowers, hung on walls above the places where they had fallen, shot as the Germans left Paris.

There seemed to us to be no shortage of food. The first night we were in Paris, I ate a month's English ration of meat at a restaurant in St. Germain. I had ordered steak tartare. I thought I knew what it was. Steak I remembered. *Tartare* meant it would have, I hoped, a tartar sauce. It arrived, a great heap of raw beef—more than a month's ration. Two raw eggs, two weeks' ration. A wonderful sauce, of course. Never mind the wine. I was drunk on protein.

Paris is made memorable by the streets where you stay, the café that welcomes you. Our street that first time was the Rue St. Louis en L'Ile, on the Ile St. Louis, downriver from the Ile de la Cité, where the back of the Cathedral of Notre Dame rose against the sky. We stayed in a hotel called the Normandie. It was four stories high and one room wide. It cost two hundred fifty of the old francs a night, about a dollar. We were on the third floor, up steep, narrow stairs. Sometime in the Third Empire, a drunken paperhanger had put the wallpaper in our room. Foot-long parrots perched in a wild Henri Rousseau jungle. The wallpaper had been put on upside down, so we woke in the morning to see, all around us, parrots standing on their heads. I picked up some French while reading *Paris Match*, the toilet paper supplied in the hall bathroom. I learned at once to say "Ça va?" instead of the polite "Comment allez-vous?" I had learned at Sweet Briar.

At first, we see what we expect in new cities. Guidebooks or novels form our expectations. I had then, as we all have, a literary memory of Paris—the Paris of Balzac, of Proust, of Huysmans, a cityscape of a time as well as a place. For the 1920s of the Americans in Paris, Hemingway is at the Ritz, Fitzgerald is drunk at midnight, Edith Wharton holds court at Fontainebleau, Djuna Barnes's *Nightwood* stands under a street lamp, Maury Paul is alive in Cat Street, and now, because of Hemingway, who was for the time as unscrupulous a tattletale as Truman Capote was later, Gertrude Stein is overheard pleading with Alice Toklas. Camus looks for a place to work unseen. Jean-Paul Sartre discovers Kierkegaard's work and acts as if he wrote it, except for Kierkegaard's leap of faith. Sartre hardly ever even crossed the Seine.

Once in a while, a very great while, we can run into a fragment of those cities of words, lost in time, and it meets the reality of our own discovered city—Pie Corner of Dickens, the Bastille, the Florence of James, the Rome of everybody. My city of words is Proust's.

I ran into my Proustian city the first time I saw Paris, the first morning. Every morning at five o'clock, horses were driven along the narrow street just below our window, to an *abattoir* in a broken-down Renaissance *hôtel de ville* with a large courtyard. The clatter of their hooves echoed against the buildings. They sounded like war horses fifteen feet high.

Later in the morning, I walked along our street and found the house of the same time, the same general layout, as the house of the Duke and Duchess de Guermantes, where Proust's family had an apartment when he was still a boy. There were the carvings, the magnificence, the long windows, one of which had been broken and covered with a board. Marcel may have watched from that window to see the magnificent Duchess de Guermantes enter her carriage. But in my *hôtel de ville*, the courtyard was red with rills of blood flowing to the central grating amid the stained stones. The air around the building smelled of raw flesh. The flies were thick.

The first floor of our hotel was a café where almost the whole of the front was opened out into the street. When we heard the metal curtain being raised, we knew we could get coffee for breakfast. Usually we shared coffee and bananas and croissants with John Cage, who lived and played music on the second floor below us. We lived in the third-floor room, and Ellsworth Kelly lived and painted in the fourth-floor room above us.

Across the street was a patisserie where a woman who didn't like anybody made wonderful croissants. She also sold bananas. So each morning we took turns braving her bad temper and asked slowly for "*Quatre croissants, quatre bananes, s'il vous plaît.*" Sometimes she refused to understand us and reduced us to pointing. It made her happy. For a French minute. She understood, depending on the moment, depending on whether it was raining or she had quarreled with her husband or was hating foreigners more than ever that day. Sometimes she pretended not to hear me and I would stand there pleading, "*Je vous en prie, madame, quatre croissants et quatre bananes.*"

In the evening, we walked to the Royale, the café across Boulevard St. Germain from the Deux Magots. It was the meeting arena for artists in Paris on the GI bill. It had been chosen with great purity by the people who took us there, and we were instructed to look down on the people at the Magots, who we were told were mostly that new breed of American cat, graduate students, and groupies looking for famous people. So the china *franc* saucers piled high, and we talked—talk that, for me, went on wonderfully through the night.

I remember talk in Paris then as continuous. I took it back to London to sustain me until the next release into Paris. The café changed, as did the street, the hotel, during the next six years. But the talk did not. There was little true conversation then in London, not like that, not those easy hours. London's so-called literary world was far too self-conscious. People seemed always to be jockeying for position, as they had done in Shakespeare's time, and Dr. Johnson's, and still do today. In Paris, the ones I knew and have been fond of ever since were far too arrogant to give a damn.

Two of the best people I have ever met who were of that curious world that outsiders and graduate students call "art," were John Cage and Ellsworth Kelly. John spoke in interrogatives: "My name's John Cage? I want to start a group called Capitalists Incorporated so it won't be banned by the Un-

American Activities Committee? To be president you have to destroy a mechanical recorder? You can be a vice-president if you destroy a record player? I want everybody to make their own music, even if it's only toilet paper on a comb?" He was a sweet, generous man, which is why I remember him beyond all the rest from that first time in Paris.

On the morning that he and Merce Cunningham, who lived in a flat on the left side of the island, were leaving for New York, we sat in the café helping Merce wait. Merce was worried, then fidgety, then fit to be tied. John had disappeared and his bags were not packed. The boat train would leave at noon.

That morning it was raining in Paris. I think it rains harder and with more personal anger in Paris than in any other city in Europe. Ten thirty came, and through the rain sloshed John, beatific looking, as if he had been totally immersed like a Baptist. His hair was plastered to his face. His raincoat was soaked and dripping.

Before Merce could say a word, John said, "I've just been listening to the sweetest music this side of heaven? I woke up this morning and realized how welcome I had been by Radio Diffusion and by the musical world of Paris while young French composers had no entrée? So I decided to take an unknown young French composer around and introduce him?" Then he said to us, and to Eduardo Paolozzi, who had joined us, "You are invited to hear his music?"

He gave us the address, and later we climbed one of those stairways where the dim light went off before you got to the next floor and the next light. In what I remember as a small room with a narrow bed and an upright piano with some of the ivory missing from the keys, the young composer played for us. His name was Pierre Boulez.

John left a record of his own for us, and we went to a record store in the Rue des Beaux Arts and asked to play it. While it was playing, I went up to the counter to thank the owner. He was talking with a customer. This was the conversation I overheard:

"Qu'est-ce que c'est?"

"C'est le bebop Chinois."

So this is one of my Parises. There were many.

This Paris of mine came back the way it should have for me, in a Proustian moment, or better, the parody of a Proustian moment. Not with a madeleine but with the taste of a bad soup. And, by the way, Proust's famous leap of memory was not a madeleine dipped in lime tea but rather a zwieback dipped in the strong morning tea full of milk when he was a child. So imagination works from the flotsam of our minds.

My found recipe was called "a simple French soup": potatoes, kale, onions, water, a mean drip of oil, parsley, and salt and pepper. Water soup. I took one taste and began to laugh. I was in a different place and in a different time, as alive, as immediate as the kitchen I sat in—the Prix Fixe in the Rue Jacob in 1949. The lunch consisted of a small piece of fish, two potatoes, a salad made of two slices of tomato with a drip of oil and vinegar, and a glass of Fetish wine from Algiers, which cost twenty-five old francs a liter. You got ten francs back on the bottle. So with the dollar at two hundred fifty francs, you can imagine the quality of the wine. Eduardo Paolozzi, now Sir Eduardo, a famous sculptor, was turning a drooping slice of tomato over and over with his fork, saying, "Next stop the river."

Twenty years later, Eduardo took me to dinner when I returned to London after many years. We went to Bentley's, the most elegant fish restaurant in London. We ate a piece of fish, two small potatoes, and a salad, and we divided a bottle of

wine—this time not from poverty but because we were both trying to lose weight. The cost would have kept us in our Paris for
a week.

In memory, cities do not change; the vision of them is
timeless, like lines of poetry. They are personal. They reflect
your friends, when you were there, and why you were there. I
never lived in Paris. We lived in London then so the memories cling together as a single time when they cover several
years. But like dreams, slips and falls of time and scenes are
tangled. I remember them as one time, in one city, the first
time I saw Paris.

My Paris is personal and unknown. It is small, too hard to
find streets where conversations and friends are remembered
on any turning into them forever after. My Paris is the Paris
of being unpublished and broke, living in tiny rooms in
hotels with laundry in the tin bidets, and having parties
where we drank Fetish that you could have used as ink. A
back street where I walked alone and an enormous Senegalese
soldier stopped me, thinking or hoping I was a whore. In the
streetlight, he was the blackest man I had ever seen, and I
thought at once, "All American black people are not black.
They are my cousins." And then I tried to remember enough
French to get me out of the situation without hurting his
feelings. I said, "J'ai du mal." He turned and walked away.
Later I found that I had told him I had syphilis. St. Sulpice,
where Max Steele and I walked along, he holding my arm
because I was still stunned from having had my first novel
accepted. Following us, jeering, were Alfred Chester, Jean Garrigue, and some others who are dim, out of the light of memory. "They won't walk with us," Alfred called, "because they
have publishers and we haven't. They're telling each other
secrets they don't want us to know." Max was speaking softly,

giving me financial advice. "If you make a little money, put it in a liquor store," he was saying. "That way, even with a depression you won't lose it."

I am hidden in a back bedroom of the Hotel Helvetia. My first novel is coming out and I am terrified. I have brought one book to Paris with me. It is *Life on the Mississippi*. I read it over and over. Alfred Chester walks in. He says he has had the best day's work ever, two thousand words. He is writing a story called "The Head of a Sad Angel." It will be the best short story I have ever read.

A few days later, I have to go back to London and face the fact that I am completely ignored. I am on the train at the Gare St. Lazare and the train is making those pulsing noises, ready to start. Max Steele runs down the platform, waving the London Sunday papers and a bottle of watermelon pickle his mother has sent him. I settle back with the papers. Fine reviews of *The Love Eaters* are carried in every London paper. A Walter Mitty dream.

Even among us, unknown, unsung, but not, God knows, silent or meek, there was a snobbery, probably forgotten by all except me. Our first publications were in either the *Paris Review* or *Botteghe Oscure*. *Botteghe* was thought to be grander than the *Paris Review*. The yet-unknown immortals published there, all brilliant, are mostly dead now. The others, myself included, published our first stories in the *Paris Review*.

We meet forever at the Café Tournon, a mom-and-pop café, cheaper than most, around the corner from the *Paris Review* office. I am huddled for hours against one of those freezing April days, sitting on a banquette in the corner at the café in the Rue de Tournon, reading a manuscript of a new book called *Watt*, or was it *Molloy*? It begins with a man trying to move five pebbles from his left pocket to his mouth to his right pocket and over again without repeating. Someone sits down beside me. I say, "Bonjour," with my mouth full of pebbles.

Three of us—Jean Garrigue and Alfred and I—walked to see the towers of Notre Dame bathed by floodlights at night. The towers seemed to grow out of the light toward heaven. Huddled in front of the hot floodlights on the ground were what at first looked like bundles of old clothes. They were the *clochards* of Paris, the homeless, the idiots, asleep in the warmth of the lights. Alfred watched them. I never saw him look up. Jean's eyes were on the towers; "so beautiful," she said, over and over. I see them both, one looking up and one down, in the floodlights of the cathedral, all of it together, poverty, poetry, pity on Alfred's face, talent and heavenly visions on Jean's, and I do not forget it.

But the greatest Proustian moment came then at the Paris flea market, which was, in those days just after the war, stalls in an open field. It was as if Odette's clothes, her silk dishabille embroidered with butterflies, her ball gowns, her hats, had been flung along the stalls or hung moving in the wind. It had been fifty years since Swann had watched her window at night, and the Japanese fashions of the turn of the century had finally reached the flea market.

A few years ago, I went back to Paris, this time with my husband, Widdy Tazewell.[1] The Rue de Tournon was a fashionable street of very expensive restaurants and shops, rare books, jewelry, and elegant apartments behind the façades of the old buildings that had once been cheap hotels or prix-fixe apartments lived in by the poor. The only place left unchanged was the Café Tournon, old and scruffy and full of ghosts. We went

---

[1] In September 1978, Mary Lee Settle married William Littleton "Widdy" Tazewell (1933–98), a columnist and historian from Norfolk, Virginia, who was teaching at the University of Virginia in Charlottesville.—AHF.

in and sat on the same banquette. I pointed out where I had talked with Max, sat with Alfred, drunk coffee with George Plimpton; I talked and talked about the past alive around me. When we left, Widdy named it the Café Déjà Vu.

We went to the flea market. It was in a permanent building, all sense of discovery lost to gimcrack objects for tourists—all except the dresses, the evening dresses with their bias cut, the small-waisted taffetas, the puffed sleeves swaying in the wind, all the fine fashions I had worn when I went to Sweet Briar and was what we called then a "prom trotter." It had been fifty years, and at last my youth had reached the Paris flea market.

EPILOGUE

❧

On the boat train from Paris back to London, Mary Lee read and reread the glowing reviews of *The Love Eaters* in the Sunday *Observer* and *The Times,* savoring them as vindication of hard choices she had made since crossing her "Rubicon," that iron-lace bridge over the Kanawha River, in 1938.

More good reviews followed the next week. "It was the most complete acceptance of a 'first novel' that anyone could dream of. I had the satisfaction of holding in my hands several cables from American editors, from publishing houses that had refused my book at reader level. I chose Harper."[1]

The same two publishers, Heinemann in London and Harper in New York, promptly published *The Kiss of Kin* (1955) as her "second" novel, and the critics praised it also. Then the book she had begun in the British Museum Reading Room long before her first novel was published, *O Beulah Land,* was brought out, by Viking in New York and Heinemann in London, in September 1956.

It was the first book written in a series of five intercon-

---

[1] Mary Lee Settle, *Contemporary Authors Autobiography Series,* vol. 1, ed. Dedria Bryfonski. Detroit: Gale Research Company, 1984, p. 316 [hereafter, *CAAS*].

nected novels spanning three hundred years of social history in
what is now West Virginia ("Beulah Land" in her fiction). The
series would be known as the Beulah Quintet, and she would
not finish it for another twenty-six years.

Although *O Beulah Land* was well received by the critics,
some expressed surprise that Settle, who had clearly mastered
modern social satire in her first two books, would now take
such a radical turn in form. The historical novel requires
months or years of research before the first sentence can be put
on paper, and the genre was generally disdained by critics at
that time.

Why did she do it? Because it was a challenge. Because there
was a question that she felt compelled to answer, and that
question forced her to go back into the past, deep into the
roots of her own society. Mary Lee Settle often said that the
source of a new novel was, for her, usually an image that pro-
voked a question. And that "why," she said, "must detonate,
like a fuse, the long, sustained, exhausting answer that is a
work of art."[2]

Her almost overnight success as a writer, her Walter Mitty
dream-come-true, put a strain on her marriage. Previously, Den
had been the teacher and she "follower" and "learner." More-
over, during the summer of 1955, when she and Christopher
were visiting her parents in West Virginia, they arranged for her
to meet again the "still . . . attractive bachelor whom they had
chosen for me years before."

"I had lived," she wrote in her 1984 autobiographical essay,
"such a hard-working, self-denying life, which demanded the
sacrifice of the ease that is the reward for social acquiescence,
that I was completely vulnerable. I fell in love. It was one of the

[2] *CAAS.*

few times since I had grown up that my father was happy about me. I don't think he ever considered that it would break up a marriage, years of English friendships, and a shakily constructed foundation of professional life. None of that existed in the world he demanded I live in."[3]

She and Den stayed together, legally, another year, long enough for him to get the papers that he needed to emigrate to the United States (where he became the much-esteemed curator, then director, of the Museum of Primitive Art in Manhattan). They were divorced late in 1956.

By that time, Mary Lee had returned to the scenes of her childhood and had begun the love affair she would portray thirty years later in the novel *Charley Bland* (1989).

A serious student of Mary Lee Settle's life story should begin by reading *Addie: A Memoir* (1998), not only for the social history of the Kanawha Valley and a vivid portrait of her maternal grandmother but also for the tensions in the complex family that shaped the child Mary Lee and haunted the adult.

Then the reader might go on to *The Clam Shell* (1971), for a fictional account of her traumatic eighteenth year at Sweet Briar College. After that, he or she would be prepared to respond to all of the nuances in the early chapters of *Learning to Fly*.

For greater detail and a different take on Settle's thirteen months in the WAAF, there is *All the Brave Promises: Memories of Aircraft Woman 2nd Class 2146391* (1966), the little book that former *Times Literary Supplement* editor Alan Pryce Jones called "one of the few really good books to come out of the Second World War."

Charley Bland (1989) carries the life story forward from

[3] *CAAS.*

1955 to 1961 in thinly disguised fiction, centering on her affair with the reckless but charming bachelor she had admired from a distance as a child. Ironically, he was the first man in her life who had ever pleased her parents. Though the novel is set five years later than the actual experience, it reflects the time that Settle spent in West Virginia, when she was in her late thirties and early forties, trying vainly to reclaim a personal life there. She was also researching and writing the second and third volumes of what she saw then as a Beulah trilogy.

In her order of priorities as a writer, telling the story of her own life was always less important than accomplishing the goal she set for herself in the early 1950s, when she began to search for the seeds of our democracy in the British Museum Reading Room.

Over the next half century, she would continue to trace, in both fiction and nonfiction, the growth of the ideas of justice, equality, and individual freedom as they were transferred from seventeenth-century England to America and then to other cultures, as the focus of her work became increasingly international. Periodically, she would turn to autobiography, almost as a form of recreation, between the long bouts of research and writing that produced the other books.

Christopher Weathersbee believes that his mother was intending to bring her life story all the way up to the twenty-first century, working on it off and on between deadlines and publicity tours for more pressing projects, most recently *I, Roger Williams* (2001) and *Spanish Recognitions* (2004).

Altogether, Mary Lee Settle managed to produce more than twenty books, including the five novels that comprise what is generally considered her masterpiece, the Beulah Quintet, and *Blood Tie* (1977), a novel about expatriates in Turkey that won the National Book Award in 1978. For Mary Lee, that presti-

gious award put an end to fourteen years of almost total neglect by the New York critics following their rejection of *Fight
Night on a Sweet Saturday* in 1964. Mary Lee, herself, came to see
Fight Night as an abortive attempt to bring the Beulah story into
the middle of the twentieth century, so almost twenty years
later, she reworked the material and expanded it in *The Killing
Ground* (1982).

During those years of neglect, Mary Lee survived by making
the most of the small advances from her publishers and her
salary from teaching one semester every year at Bard College in
upstate New York. By living frugally, she managed to support
herself through the research and writing of six more books.
Two of them were books for younger readers, *The Story of Flight*
(1967) and *The Scopes Trial: The State of Tennessee v. John Thomas
Scopes* (1972). The other four were major works: the memoir *All
the Brave Promises* (1966) and the novels *The Clam Shell* (1971),
Prisons (1973), which takes the Beulah saga back to its beginning in a churchyard in seventeenth-century England, and
finally, after three years spent in Turkey, *Blood Tie* (1977).

When Mary Lee won the National Book Award for *Blood Tie*,
her literary reputation sprang back to life. The publisher's
advances increased by a multiple of seven, and the reviews of
her next two books—*The Scapegoat* (1980) and *The Killing Ground*
(1982)—appeared on the front page of *The New York Times Book
Review*. The year 1978 also brought a revolution in her personal
life with her marriage in September to William "Widdy"
Tazewell, a historian and journalist fifteen years her junior, who
was teaching at the University of Virginia. He would be her constant companion, editor, and booster until his death in 1998.

The novelist and poet (and Mary Lee's close friend) George
Garrett followed her roller-coaster ride with the critics through
the years and wrote a penetrating analysis of her life's work—

until the late 1980s—in *Understanding Mary Lee Settle* (University of South Carolina Press, 1988). It is well worth reading, although it does not cover the later work: *Charley Bland* (1989); her much-praised travel book, *Turkish Reflections: A Biography of a Place* (1991); the wonderful novel *Choices* (1995)—whose plucky heroine's passionate commitment to political and social ideals was equaled only by the author's; *Addie: A Memoir* (1998); *I, Roger Williams* (2001); and *Spanish Recognitions: The Roads to the Present* (2004).

By the winter of 2004–5, when cancer finally broke through the iron discipline with which Settle had managed to protect her sacred writing time for more than fifty years—radically reducing it but never, for a single day, totally destroying it—she considered this memoir, *Learning to Fly*, virtually finished.

It would have taken her only a few weeks to pull together the chapters scattered on her laptop, then finish writing the fragments, "Coronation" and "Nine Years," and, if she felt it necessary, work into the rhythm of the main text the essays on Eliot, Maugham, and her visits to Paris.

And after all, as her son observes, she was "intending to live to be a hundred and twenty."[4] So there would be plenty of time to put the final polish on this memoir, once she had captured from her still-teeming brain a first draft of the book she felt compelled to write on the boyhood of Thomas Jefferson.

With the latter goal in mind, in August 2004 Mary Lee moved out of the small house by the bean field in Kinsale, Virginia—where she had written all of *Spanish Recognitions* and most of *Learning to Fly*—and settled into another one, on Decca

---

[4] Christopher Weathersbee, conversation with Anne Hobson Freeman, June 21, 2006. As late as June 2005, Mary Lee still thought that she had licked the cancer, but in July she learned that what she called "the little weasel" had metastasized in her brain.—AHF.

Lane, in Ivy, just outside of Charlottesville, to continue work
on the new book. It was tentatively entitled *Tom*; she had begun
it during a three-month residency, from October 2003 through
December 2003, at the Thomas Jefferson Library at Monticello.

Though bedridden, and almost blind at the end, she was
still struggling to finish *Tom* with the help of an intern, her son
Christopher, and a host of volunteers when she lost her fight
with cancer on September 27, 2005.

On the wall beside her bed—next to the huge map of the ter-
rain of Jefferson's boyhood that Mary Lee kept there—a friend
had tacked up a clipping that Mary Lee cherished. It was from
the *San Francisco Chronicle*, quoting the historian David McCul-
lough on the desire to keep on learning that drove them both:

> That's exactly why I do what I do. Learn new things.
> Find out. Do you know Mary Lee Settle's books? Won-
> derful historical novelist. I heard her give a talk at Mon-
> ticello once and she said, "I write to find out." That's it!
> You can't say it any simpler.[5]

Mary Lee told Matthew Bruccoli that she hoped that her
last book, *Tom*, would be "the crown of my whole life's work."
Even after she had finished the Beulah Quintet, she explained:

> I still didn't find how we got the separation of church
> and state. So I wrote about Roger Williams. Now, I'm
> writing about what came into the mind of a gangling 9-
> to 14-year-old in a frontier county, who had had to live
> with rich relations up till the time he was nine. Who
> was surrounded by dissenters, so the first thing that he,

[5] Edward Guthmann, *San Francisco Chronicle*, June 27, 2005.

when he grew up and went into the House of Burgesses, the first thing he wrote about was the separation of church and state. You know who I'm talking about? It's Jefferson as a boy. . . . I must find out how it came to somebody, who when he grew up was able to sit down and write the Declaration of Independence. . . . I want to finish that book and die of sheer joy with my head on the manuscript.[6]

And she almost did.

—Anne Hobson Freeman

---

[6] Matthew J. Bruccoli, "Die of Sheer Joy," Mary Lee Settle Interviews, *Appalachian Heritage*, Winter 2006, pp.96–97.

APPENDIX
A GLIMPSE OF *TOM*

Only death could cancel Mary Lee Settle's commitment to re-create the world of Thomas Jefferson's boyhood; it caught her long before she had finished her first draft. She had hoped, of course, that *Tom* would be her final answer to the questions that had driven her to write the Beulah Quintet and *I, Roger Williams*—questions about the origins of our democracy.

For Mary Lee, the writing of historical fiction was a calling. And once it overtook her in the British Museum in the early 1950s, she followed it with an almost fanatical devotion for half a century—through good reviews and bad reviews, prosperity and poverty, and even, at the end, debilitating illness.

In a proposal to her editor in 2004, she explained it this way:

> Perhaps some history of The Beulah Quintet is useful, since I came to Norton after it had been in print for some time, and since this book about Jefferson's childhood is, to me, its culmination. I do not write "what I know." I write to find a reliable answer to the question that haunts me until I do.
>
> I had written two modern novels, neither of which

was yet published, when I was struck hard with a subject that has demanded ever since that I find the true answer to certain questions. The questions have grown as I have worked.

First, I wanted to find the realities of our past that I knew to be so over-laden with the censorship of dependence on slanted legal documents, communal memory, and protective legend that the reality of who we were and what we have become is obscured by them.

I wanted to take our history back to the time when shelter and food were a luxury to root, hog, or die for. Above all I wanted to try to become contemporary with the people of the time and find out what they thought and above all what they took for granted, for it is that which we inherit.

O Beulah Land, which examines life in Virginia in the mid-eighteenth century, came first. The research was done in the British Museum, which was a gold mine for me; the vast majority of books, articles, etc., were published in England; the laws were made there. Above all, most of the immigrants who came to Virginia were English, with a minority of Irish and Scottish people.

I never went, in final research, beyond 1774, since I realized that subtleties of language change were affected by revolution. I started in 1763, at the end of the Seven Years War which we call the French and Indian War. Because the main impetus for immigration was land hunger, I used the hymn "O Beulah Land" as the title. (*"I look away across the sea, where mansions are prepared for me, and view the shining glory shore, my heaven, my home forevermore."*)

It is the research for that volume which will be so valuable for the book about Jefferson's youth since it covers the same time, the pre-revolutionary eighteenth century.

This was followed in sequence with *Know Nothing*, which ended as the American Civil War began. *The Scapegoat*, which came next, was about the growing quarrel between capital and labor in the early twentieth century, ending with what I thought at the time was the ending, *The Killing Ground*.

The story still would not let me go. I had not yet asked the two most important questions of all. Two revolutionary ideas about governing—democracy, and the separation of church and state—were first implemented here on these shores. How did they get here? What brain brought them? Who articulated them? Who first brought the idea of the separation of church and state here in the seventeenth century when no country "in all the world" accepted it?

It was the basis for *Prisons*, which, though written last, was the story of the influence of the English Civil Wars on our thinking and many of our immigrants.

I found Roger Williams, about whom I, like too many modern Americans, knew almost nothing, and became so his spokesperson and his brother that when I look at *I, Roger Williams* now, I literally don't know where his voice leaves off and mine begins.

Now I find that the culmination of my whole life's work is this question: How did his times, his surroundings and the adults he looked up to, and the past he inherited help to form the mind and attitudes of Jefferson? One of the deficiencies in American studies of the life of Thomas Jefferson (as with Roger Williams) is that they begin too late, as if the subject's mind had sprung full grown without being influenced, and without learning.

Jefferson was born only eighty years after the end of the English Civil Wars which had a profound effect on the American colonies, when immigrants brought the pros and cons of the war to Virginia. Those who were transported, for either political or legal reasons, represented both sides of the conflict (see volume 1 of The Beulah Quintet, *Prisons*). [They were a mixture of] Cromwellians, Royalists who fled after losing the war, and especially important in Jefferson's case, since later he was to quote them, the Levellers, the extreme representatives of democracy as an idea for governing who also had to flee Cromwell.

That polyglot was the great grandfather's generation to those born in the early to mid-eighteenth century. We all know that our own Civil War is still very much alive after a hundred and fifty years; we in the South especially who were born in the first quarter of the twentieth century know how alive it was after only fifty or sixty years. (I was christened by my great grandfather, a preacher who had fought with the 33rd Virginia Infantry.) It was a southerner, William Faulkner, who wrote, "The past is not dead. It isn't even past."[1]

As a coda to her memoir about writing, *Learning to Fly*, excerpts from Mary Lee's final flight, *Tom*, are published below

---

[1] Mary Lee Settle, computer files, "Miscellaneous, CHILDHOOD4, August 14, 2004."

with the hope that they may inspire some future writer to take up the task where she was forced to leave it.

Her son remembers that the day before she died, she was still working on it, looping giant letters with a black felt pen in one of the six large artist's sketch books she was using by that time.[2] The last section of her manuscript contains the following entry:[3]

Notes on Tom—for someone to continue, with deepest apologies from me because I can't finish.

Tom is now nine. He has grown into an un[gainly], contemplative child whose powerful, inquiring mind is already *big*. [He is] beginning to react to his world. Think of the grown man who (*if there are lacunae it is because I can't see well and am lying in the hospital, and must take off again where the thought has been interrupted*). The major clue that connected the child to the man was in the visit from [the Marquis de Chastellux]. In it he wrote that Jefferson was [serious] and cold but as soon as they could get to know each other (it only took the first—probably—day), Jefferson became—*I'm sorry, I must continue this when I can have a magnifying glass.*

The facts are known. They have never been connected. Wordsworth wrote not long after Jefferson's death, "The child is father of the man." In that story that [Chastellux] wrote there are reflections, all the way through Jefferson's volumes of letters sometimes small clues to find—he writes to a friend when they are in college or studying law with [George Wythe] at Williams-

2 Christopher Weathersbee, conversation with Anne Hobson Freeman, April 6, 2007.
3 Mary Lee's comments to the reader are in italics; editorial clarifications are bracketed.

burg, that they must work out a secret code—so that
they won't be [teased about what they write] (*I have forgotten the exact words*). . . . [T]hey go back to scene after
scene of his childhood, and it is a common scene with
so many. . . . the rejection of the extremely intelligent
when they are children—see the modern language—
geek, nerd—and the pure hatred of the attacked [want-
ing to return the attack] in kind—usually intelligently.
. . . [T]he intelligence turns to violence when it attacks
[to the] point of no return. Fortunately the child whose
social intelligence is developed survives this and
becomes loving and compassionate toward those with
less talent . . . and [those] more socially arrested at an
almost tribal level. Jefferson [w]as a boy, who learned to
. . . trust a few friends and who was able to learn to
become a politic person as he grew up; [he] survived the
period of masked reaction—but the hatred of the rich
stayed with him while he learned to hide his warm self
behind a protective façade.[4]

On Mary Lee's computer were blocks of finished text,
including one that might have served as the opening. It presents the boy of nine who has just returned with his family to
Shadwell,[5] their own small house on the edge of the frontier,

---

[4] Mary Lee Settle, *Tom*, unpublished manuscript, Book VI.
[5] Shadwell, Thomas Jefferson's birthplace, was three miles east of present-day
Charlottesville in Albemarle County, Virginia. Soon after Peter Jefferson pur-
chased the Shadwell tract in 1741, he built the house in which his oldest son,
Thomas, spent much of his early life. When the Shadwell house (and all of the
documents it contained) burned to the ground in 1770, Thomas Jefferson
moved to Monticello, which was already under construction. John T. Salmon,
compiler, *A Guidebook to Virginia's Historical Markers* (Charlottesville: University of
Virginia Press, 2007), p. 93.

after seven years spent living with rich relatives farther east at the Randolphs' plantation, Tuckahoe:[6]

The Boy Jefferson

The childhood shows the man
As morning shows the day.

Paradise Regained. John Milton[7]

Tom Jefferson did not know the home he loved so until he was nine years old. He was to love it all of his life, the place to which he always referred simply as "the mountain" as if it were the center of the world, and for him, it was. He longed for it when he was abroad, whether in the east of the colony, or in Europe. He was taken away from it two years after his birth, and all he remembered of it until he was nine was being cradled by one of his father's two slaves on a horse.

The family, his three sisters, his mother and his father, were moving east to the plantation of a relative of his mother's, to whom his father was conscious of owing too much to refuse his dying request: that he would come and run his huge plantation until his eldest son was of age. [That relative] was William Ran-

---

[6] Tuckahoe, an H-shaped plantation house, "perhaps the oldest frame residence on [the] James River west of Richmond, . . . was begun about 1715 by Thomas Randolph," grandfather of the orphaned Thomas Randolph for whose sake the Jefferson family lived at Tuckahoe for seven years. The little schoolhouse where the later Thomas Randolph and his cousin Tom Jefferson studied as children still stands there. Salmon, *Guidebook to Virginia's Historical Markers,* p. 122.

[7] Epigram from Settle, computer files, "Miscellaneous, CHILDHOOD4, August 14, 2004."

dolph, [Peter Jefferson's dearest friend] one of [those] whom later the boy would call, ironically, the "Eastern Grandees." He obviously learned early to be not only shy of it, but critical of the daily way of life, so admired by the colonial society, and he would refer to it with some contempt.

The tutor in the little one-roomed school the children of William Randolph and the children of Peter Jefferson attended until the boy was nine was an unqualified teacher, and the boy knew it. He had learned to read early, learned to listen while seemingly withdrawn, a quality noticed by his school mates later. A child too bright learns to hide it, to hide a questioning mind for safety's sake. He sensed what was incompetent, dangerous, and, worse to him, foolish. This boy, Tom Jefferson, seems to have learned to hide his opinions until they burst out in passionate abstractions that would change an English colony into a nascent country. The ugly duckling knows it, no matter how proud his father [is] of him, no matter how indifferent his mother. He knew early to watch and wait and listen, and that he was an other, born a stranger in a familiar world. He learned to love his friends, and keep to himself.

A child knows early, too, that the place of his own family in such a position in an isolated community is looked on as a subservient one. The Randolph family made no bones about their opinion that their cousin, the boy's mother, had married beneath her. Growing older in such a community of women, in a "grandee" colonial atmosphere, it was inevitable that the boy would pick up clues to what they considered was his father's place in the world.

He adored his father. All his life he spoke of him with pride. And well he may have done, for his father was showing, beyond the social confines of one plantation, a talent and a technical brilliance that brought him into contact and earned him the respect of the small ruling community of Virginia.[8]

The clash of cultures within the boy's mind, and the love for his father, would affect his attitudes for the rest of his life. It was with pride that he spoke of his father as self-taught; there was no apology about it. His father, to him, was the new world, opening up as he grew.

For a reason which I have not found so far, but which I suspect, the withdrawal of the boy, perhaps the unhappiness of his mother, made the father decide not to honor any longer his friend's request. When the boy was nine, and his [older] sisters were in their adolescence, he took them back west to the frontier county where they had been born.[9]

There his father had earned the respect and honor that he was to have for the rest of his life. It was the respect of a strong, dependable, richly talented man, who, like his neighbors, had begun to carve out a farm

[8] Peter Jefferson had been hired as a surveyor by Joshua Fry, who was professor of mathematics at the College of William and Mary in Williamsburg and, after 1740, Peter's neighbor in Albemarle County. Fry and Peter Jefferson had become partners and in 1751 completed the famous Fry-Jefferson "Map of the Most Inhabited part of Virginia. . . ." based on detailed land measurements and river surveys.—AHF.

[9] By this time, Tom had four sisters—two older, Jane (b. 1740) and Mary (b. 1741), and two younger, Elizabeth (b. 1744) and Martha (b. 1746). Two infant brothers, born in 1748 and 1750, had died at Tuckahoe. After the family's return to Shadwell, three more siblings would be born: Lucy in 1752, and the twins, Anna Scott and Randolph, in 1755. Dumas Malone, *The Young Jefferson* (Boston: Little Brown, 1941), p. 430.

in the wilderness. In the western foothills of the tower-
ing unknown mountains, a community was being
slowly born.[10]

This relatively polished text is followed by a series of discon-
nected fragments found in the 8½″ × 11″ Canson artist's sketch
books, numbered one through six, in which Mary Lee wrote the
drafts of *Tom*, in increasingly large letters, when she was no longer
able to work on a computer. Three of those fragments—though
rough and incomplete, with words that could not be transcribed
deleted—are printed below to give at least a hint of the book that
Tom might have been had its author lived to finish it:

Who could have known that this one obscure boy from
an obscure county in the Crown Colony of Virginia was
endowed with one of those rare priceless questioning
minds whose fallow field is preparing him with what he
hears, what he sees, above all what he questions. . . .
    Tom, without knowing it, had such a mind, that of
Galileo, of Aristotle . . . those rare ones who carried
within themselves when they were children the fallow
fields that are called genius. (From MS Book I)

AT TUCKAHOE, THE REVEREND STITH
INTERVIEWS TOM, AGE SEVEN
(MS Book III):
For four years the Randolph cousins in their legions
had been accusing Peter Jefferson of stealing the [Ran-
dolph] boy's money.[11]

---

[10] Settle, computer files, "Miscellaneous, CHILDHOOD1, July 9, 2004."
[11] The boy referred to in this sentence is Thomas Randolph, the heir to Tuckahoe, whose father, William Randolph, at the time of his death, had asked his

The Reverend Stith for all that time had been plagued about it until his wife, Thomas's aunt, persuaded him to look into the matter. He didn't believe a word of it. William had left the two soberest, in both senses, men he knew, to care for Thomas, and the boy seemed happy enough even though he was a bit slower than the Reverend Stith had hoped. But then, the only comparison for the quality of his care and his teaching had been this tall weedy seven-year-old who stood in front of him. He found the boy disconcerting. He looked straight into the Reverend Stith's eyes, as if he had gone beyond politeness and good manners.

"Can you read, young man?" the Reverend Stith asked, and settled his body back comfortingly into the most comfortable chair in the library to do his duty and satisfy his wife. He had, after all, just retired from being the president of the College of William and Mary in Williamsburg so nobody could have been better qualified. A breeze wandered into the window and gave a minute's promise to lift the heat when the sun went down. He sighed.

This gawky gangling boy with his flyaway red hair and his adult eyes still watched him and waited.

"I think you had better find something to read to me."

---

friend Peter Jefferson and his brother-in-law, the Reverend Stith, to be guardians of his son until he came of age. Thomas Randolph was two years older than Tom Jefferson. In this passage, the Reverend Stith is interviewing the younger boy, Tom, to judge whether or not he and his older cousin, Thomas Randolph, were being educated properly at Tuckahoe.

The rumors that Peter Jefferson was mismanaging the funds were apparently unfounded but were obviously hurtful to the Jefferson family.—AHF.

Tom thought for a minute and then picked up the nearest book. It was one of his very favorites. *Don Quixote.* "The innkeeper," he read in a near whisper.

"Speak up, boy," the Reverend commanded. He was a little deaf. When Tom raised his voice, it disappeared up the scale and into a squeak and then silence, then returned to a whisper again. The voice did not match the adult eyes.

". . . seeing Don Quixote slung across the ass, asked Sancho what was amiss with him." A near whisper again.

"Do you have any Latin?" the Reverend asked him. It was a simple thing he had been asked to do. Find out how well the boy had been taught, so he could compare him to Thomas, even though he was two years younger.

"Have you had any Latin?" he asked again, forgetting he had already asked it. It was too hot to think clearly.

When he said, "A little," [the Reverend said,] "Read and translate: *Equo ne credite, Teucri.*" Tom began.

The Reverend stopped him. "I thought you began at nine in the Latin school. Who taught you?"

"I listened while the Reverend Douglas taught Thomas, sir, so I could help him."

All in a near whisper, all with the disconcerting gaze of a child who seemed to have been alone for so long that he no longer knew it was bad manners for a child to watch his elders and betters. Not once did Tom drop his eyes in a becoming manner. Not once did he speak above a near whisper.

"Come here, young man." The Reverend suddenly changed into a peer. He patted the boy's arm. "What do you think Virgil meant when he wrote that?" He had forgotten to be an inquisitor and was enjoying himself. He, too, had had his years of having nobody to talk to.

WATCHING HIS FATHER AND HIS PARTNER, JOSHUA FRY, AT THEIR WORK (MS Book VI):

He understood his father's isolation without words or even conscious thought. He simply, when he was at home at Shadwell for the long hot summer vacation, followed him around like a pup, one six foot two inches tall, one nine years old, tall for his age, skinny as a rake. He learned his father's stride, a small imitation of the tall man. He [watched] his father and Joshua Fry [in] the small office built as an out building at Shadwell, silent, talking, his voice still a whisper, his love safe. When they surveyed in the new county, they did not "teach" him, but let wonderful facts fall his way. They let him listen.

[Looking down on the boy who was wearing] a very wide brimmed straw hat to protect his frail skin from the sun, his father said that from above he looked like a mushroom.

[The boy] ambled along behind him, seeing the world around him as if it were new born. While his father and his partner walked along, measuring the land to tame it, they talked politics as if what they saw was daily and a common thing.

The boy saw it as miraculous. His father could see beyond the horizon, away out of sight, with the aid of the beautiful instruments Tom would polish and feel as if they were alive. The world beyond was infinite and . . . knowable. He was sure of this. Miraculous, huge, and tiny as a single flower in the waist-high meadows that were gradually being cleared of the huge trees that had shaded [them like] a green wood roof that kept out most of the sun. . . . And always beyond it, the unknown to be discovered.

ACKNOWLEDGMENTS

Special thanks to Mary Lee Settle's son, Christopher Weathersbee, for assembling the text of this memoir from the files on his mother's computer, for transcribing handwritten pages of *Tom* that were illegible to others, and, most of all, for digging deep into his own memory for answers to numerous questions. I believe that Mary Lee would also want to acknowledge the constant encouragement and support she received from her dear friends from Norfolk, Kate and Stanworth Brinkley; her Kinsale landlords, Berthelle and Stephen Denton; and her beloved editor, Starling Lawrence, during the time that she was writing *Learning to Fly*.

—Anne Hobson Freeman

PHOTOGRAPH CREDITS

❦